To the students and faculty
of
Gordon College.

Paul Stroyen M.O.

www.ComeSunday.net

COME SUNDAY

Inspiration for
Living with Heart

COME SUNDAY

Inspiration for
Living with Heart

DISCARDED
JENKS LRC
GORDON COLLEGE

FOREWORD BY COACH JIM AND JULI BOEHEIM

PAUL C. STOMPER, M.D.

with Karen A. Walker

JENKS LIBRARY
GORDON COLLEGE
255 GRAPEVINE RD.
WENHAM, MA 01984

Copyright © 2006 by Paul C. Stomper

All rights reserved. No part of this book shall be reproduced or transmitted in any form or by any means, electronic, mechanical, magnetic, photographic including photocopying, recording or by any information storage and retrieval system, without prior written permission of the publisher. No patent liability is assumed with respect to the use of the information contained herein. Although every precaution has been taken in the preparation of this book, the publisher and author assume no responsibility for errors or omissions. Neither is any liability assumed for damages resulting from the use of the information contained herein.

To protect patient privacy and confidentially, any patient stories included in this work are medical narratives, accounts of real people altered somewhat, or composite stories representing multiple people, that are used as illustrative examples. No person or place can be assumed or identified unless specifically noted. No specific institutional practice or philosophy is represented.

Appropriate rights and permissions were obtained for usage of song lyrics, photographs, interviews, or direct quotes from other copyrighted sources or individuals that were not deemed fair usage or public domain. All quotes were verified when possible. See Notes and Permissions section.

ISBN 0-7414-3415-6

Published by:

INFI∞ITY
PUBLISHING.COM

1094 New DeHaven Street, Suite 100
West Conshohocken, PA 19428-2713
Info@buybooksontheweb.com
www.buybooksontheweb.com
Toll-free (877) BUY BOOK
Local Phone (610) 941-9999
Fax (610) 941-9959

Printed in the United States of America
Printed on Recycled Paper
Published July 2006

A tribute to the patients
and
dedicated staff and
employees
of cancer centers —
cancer victors.

Foreword

Through years of coaching and over 700 wins in the exciting, competitive world of college basketball, a National Championship season, induction into the Basketball Hall of Fame, marriage, children, and family life, there is always the feeling of a need for "Sunday" and the hope that "this isn't all there is." And then, there was each of the over 240 losses, put in perspective by occasional, unexpected news of premature deaths of former players, young athletes facing crises in their college, professional, and family lives, and sickness and loss among our own family and friends. During these times especially, there was the feeling of a need for "Sunday" and the hope that "this isn't all there is."

Today, successful people search for tools, aids, and anything that can give them an advantage and better perspective. In COME SUNDAY: INSPIRATION FOR LIVING WITH HEART, Dr. Paul Stomper shares a rich and powerful experience that can provide inspiration in many settings.

Two of the themes in this book...jazz music and sports...are truly universal themes and languages that express the joy and gift of living and human aspiration. COME SUNDAY portrays the inspirational power of the endeavors of athletes, coaches, and musicians. It also provides a humbling comparison of their "struggles" and aspirations with those of Dr. Stomper's "cancer victors."

Our lives have been impacted by athletes, coaches, and friends and family members who have survived or succumbed to cancer. We too, personally, have experienced a successful early diagnosis and treatment of cancer. But in our busy professional and family lives, have we fully realized the potential of the new life –giving perspective? Have we been able to share this with the people we care most about?

This book would have been an inspirational companion for us during these times. But even more, it is a book for all seasons and all people. And it is truly a book about living... and winning.

Along with other college basketball coaches and their wives, we have gained great satisfaction from our efforts with the Coaches versus Cancer Foundation. Dr. Stomper follows the late coach and cancer victim Jim Valvano's charge of "Never give up...Never ever give up" with themes such as "Live to the End. Give to the End," "Play Right Through It," "Inspiration for a Lifetime," "Life Beyond the Final Buzzer," "Follow your Heart," and the interesting twist "Invest in Your Fortune 500."

The stories and collection of quotes shared by Paul Stomper are thought-provoking. But even more, they are warm and heartening and they touch us personally. Come Sunday is an inspirational companion. At opportune times, sharing a special chapter with a friend or loved one may make a difference. Or it may simply serve as a gesture that we care and want to let someone know that "I Am With You."

The players in this rich experience are jazz musicians, athletes and coaches, and people with cancer and those that serve them -- a dream team in our hearts and minds -- and the author, who truly appreciates all of them. The message-- timeless and universal-- is for every person.

Coach Jim and Juli Boeheim
Syracuse University

... just a bunch of words and
musical notes,
unless brought to life by the
reader and listener...

INTRODUCTION

Nestled deep in every man's breast is a hope for better things to come. Each man, woman, teenager, and child hopes for more from family, friends, school, career, or work. An addict hopes for inner peace. A patient hopes for cure. An athlete hopes for victory. A peaceful man hopes for a world free from terrorism and war.

In many aspects of our ordinary daily lives we hope for "Sunday." Just as the family member, the addict, and the athlete hope for better things to come, so also an accountant, student, construction worker, waitress, mother, retail employee, actor, elected official, or CEO—at some point in each of their lives—yearns for Sunday; for welcome rest after a demanding week.

Sunday, a time to nurture things that matter most; to pray and worship, to spend time with family and friends, to put away cares and relax, to savor life and nature, to nurture and strengthen important, life-giving personal relationships.

At another, deeper level there is another hunger, another hope in the human heart—a hope for eternal permanence to the better things; a hope for no death, no end, no tears, no sorrow, no suffering, no evil…a deep yearning for pure life and joy and inner peace. Every man shares in this hope, every man. Augustine, a great thinker and writer from the 3rd century put it this way: "Our hearts are restless, until they rest in Thee, O Lord."

This inborn human yearning for life-giving Sunday, for our truest sense of home, that is what this book is all about.

The theological, philosophical, and psychological aspects of these yearnings are left to other minds versed in such things. The lives and reflections of the men and women featured in this little book are testimony of a deeper, more concrete sense of Sunday than we ever could have known without them.

But their testimony of Sunday is too important not to be shared with all, with every person. These men and women serve as different points of pure light to others, as gentle and clear gifts to each of us, as life giving, hope-filled gifts to their world of family, friends, and professional associates.

The insights come from sports figures, jazz legends, and from patients with cancer and the myriad of often nameless heroes who serve them with spirit and dedication—nurses, technologists, therapists, ministers, receptionists, secretaries, maintainance and housekeeping staff, administrators, volunteers, scientists, researchers, and doctors.

Few things give life more perspective than a diagnosis of cancer. In a single instance it touches many lives at once— family members, friends, friends of friends. Initial shock or denial quickly gives way to something much more powerful and life-giving—a stronger-than-ever appreciation for life, radical change, hope-filled transformation, and unwavering faith. These are the same characteristics of faith-appreciating athletes and jazz masters.

Amid all the demanding clinical service, cancer research, and medical journal articles that so many of my medical colleagues have poured into saving more and more lives over the past 25 years, nothing in my professional life has touched or motivated me more than the stories, snapshot vignettes and insights of the often silent victors; the patients themselves, and those who serve them.

These stories have been shared in formal talks and casual conversations. But those were select opportunities delivered to select audiences. This book is a humble attempt to share with you, dear reader, the song of the victors who surround

us daily…a weaving together of my journal notes and quotes, half-sentences and clear, sharp memories of life-changing, life-giving exchanges…of inspirational reflections from sports leaders and jazz masters, and especially from cancer victors.

These victors exemplify in a very human way the searching, exploration, and discovery portrayed in the version of Duke Ellington's jazz composition entitled "Come Sunday," played by Eric Dolphy on bass clarinet and Richard Davis on string bass.

May you discover the same vibrant and inspiring hope and life-giving song that these silent heroes have uncovered for me.

May your heart likewise resonate, *Come Sunday*…

TABLE OF CONTENTS

Eric Dolphy, 1961 ©*Val Wilmer*

One

Coltrane & Dolphy:
The Spirit of a Musician

Life...Our own life...
**a fusion of experiences...a unique collage...
...improvisation inspired by faith.**

In one sense, completely our own—
to make of it what we will...to be or achieve anything
we want to be or achieve...to follow and live our
dreams...to reach out and touch others in meaningful
ways...to love...to follow our hearts.

But...
Did we *plan* to exist? Did we bring ourselves
into being?
Were we there when the sea was formed
and the earth was made?
Do we truly have the ultimate last word?

Do we each have a unique purpose?

Maybe we don't have all the answers in life,
and maybe that's OK...
...because Somebody *does* have them all.

Many top athletes exude a sense of spirit beyond themselves
when they pour every ounce of heart, strain, and concentration
into being the best possible...The greatest among progressive jazz musicians have a sense of humility about their unique
talent, exploring chords, tones, notes and shades of sound;
curious, searching, discovering... Cancer victors—patients with
cancer and those who serve in cancer centers,

who embrace the ordinariness of life with faith—share with
these sports figures and jazz masters a sense of journey,
              of aspiration and of reaching beyond themselves...

              They believe that what they do matters,
     even if it seems small compared to what other people do,
     even if it goes unnoticed—
              a view of life that dramatically changes how these men
              and women live each day, face each challenge, and
                       embrace each moment of the journey.

              The Cancer Victors are Victors of Faith—
                   quietly challenging each of us:

Do we *really* believe in a loving God...or do we just say it?
Do we *really* believe in Easter...or do we just *say* we believe?

              Often in a quiet, matter-of-fact and real-time way—
without drawing attention to themselves, without fanfare or
preaching—these victors of faith exhibit their belief in a loving
God...in simple ways...in how they live, exhibiting calm confidence that life does not end when our mortal bodies die...in
a belief that we will live forever because death has been conquered... They walk with inner conviction about this teaching
and they never feel parted from the love of God.

              They live with a reassuring peace and hope,
                   knowing that this is not all there is...

              These silent heroes, these Victors of Faith, are all
     around us—each one manifesting God's love that surrounds
     us, every day.

How they comfort us…
How they lead us by their influence…
How they inspire us to live like they do…

Even, as John Maxwell wrote,
the most shy and introverted person
may influence 1,000 other people
in his or her lifetime…
and can be a truly virtuous leader,
a Victor of Faith.

Improvisation…jazz…life…
competitive athletics…immediate, spontaneous,
alive…searching and discovering…reaching,
stretching, ever-evolving, exploring and extending
beyond the status quo
… finding new avenues for expression.

It's about freedom, expressed in
America's original art form…jazz

…and it includes mistakes, flukes,
squeaks and mis-directions along the way.

It is human and fresh and spiritual.

Eric Dolphy and John Coltrane
were two stellar examples of this level of
jazz improvisation and aspiration, exemplary
in their intense passion for exploring sounds,
for capturing spiritual expression through music,
for searching for perfection,

continually reaching outside the box...
both single-heartedly following their hearts,
their unique paths...

Eric Dolphy grew up in the Watts section of Los Angeles.
Born in 1928, he began recording after 1959...
But his life and musical journey were cut short abruptly in 1964.
During a stint in Europe, Dolphy died unexpectedly,
in a coma from undiagnosed diabetes.
His death was described by some as "an overdose of honey,"
paying poetic tribute to
his drug-free and alcohol-free lifestyle.

Dolphy was only 36 years old.

Come Sunday

He left little material wealth. His 1961 federal income
tax return showed earnings of $4000
-- $2,394.46 in income
and $1,608.60 in royalties.

It is written that Sadie and Eric, Sr., who passed away in 1988,
told wonderful stories about their son and his early years.
An avid musician who began the clarinet at age 7,
Dolphy practiced constantly, excelling in orchestra and band.
He was chosen to play with the Los Angeles
City School Orchestra and in All-City concerts.

With dreams of being the first black principal clarinetist in a
    major U.S. Philharmonic orchestra,
      the teenager studied with legendary L.A. jazz educator
    Lloyd Reese, who had nurtured the likes of
        Charles Mingus and others.
He also studied classical music
  with the clarinet, flute, and bass clarinet,
    mastering the alto saxophone as well.
Later, Eric Dolphy played a major role in
introducing the bass clarinet into jazz music.

"A friend from [his childhood days] wrote:
    I remember Eric as a skinny kid with a clarinet case,
hurrying down West 36th Street, where he lived and his
parents still live, and having a friend tell me: 'that Eric
Dolphy is to be great someday. All he does is practice
and practice his clarinet.'"

                Eric Dolphy, A Musical Biography and Discography
                  by Vladimir Simosko & Barry Tepperman

Church and faith were integral parts of his life.
    As a young adult, Dolphy taught Sunday school at the
Westminister Presbyterian Church, where the pastor
was the father of the great jazz pianist,
Hampton Hawes. In later years, Dolphy attended
Westminster Presbyterian whenever
he was in Los Angeles.

Thoughtful and calm...introspective...searching...
curious... intense... passionate...clean-living, never
involved with drug or alcohol abuse. Dolphy was
fascinated with creating sound, with capturing new

forms of expression... He was always pushing
the envelope, not in showiness but in genuine
exploration...attentive... a gentle listener...
extraordinarily sensitive to sounds...

Captivated by the song of birds, attracted by a bird's
sense of freedom, Dolphy tried to capture that feeling in music
and played his instrument with them...

"At home [in California] I used to play,
and the birds always used to whistle with me.
I would stop what I was working on
and play with the birds." *Eric Dolphy*

"Birds have notes in between our notes—
you try to imitate something they do and...
you'll have to go up or come down on the pitch.
It's really something!... I don't know how you label
it, but it's pretty."

Eric Dolphy, interview with DownBeat

"...as I play more and more, I hear more notes
to play against the more common chord progressions.
A lot of people say they're wrong.

"Well, I can't say they're right, and I can't say
they're wrong. To my hearing, they're exactly correct...
it makes everything broader, it gives me more
things to play, it opens up a whole different type of
hearing...

music contains rhythm, and pitch, time, space,
and all these elements go into improvisation...
it's not a question of just running notes."

Dolphy, interview with Leonard Feather

Mingus recalls a party
    in Germany, in 1964:

"...while others socialized, Dolphy stood
    next to the stereo playing along with the
fast-flowing lines of a Charlie Parker record."

David Was,
"Eric Dolphy: Saintly, Selfless and Underappreciated"

But Dolphy was far from the
eccentric, non-social artist....

"...perhaps the most important thing about Eric was
    that he was a fine person, a gentle gentleman of a
    man, a person whose curiosity about everything led
    him into every kind of social milieu and whose warm
    friendliness made him welcome...
In the end, every man is seen as a human being.
    Brilliant musician that he was,
        Eric was still greater as a person.
He was thoughtful, gracious, and
        genuinely interested in others...
He knew how to enjoy what came his way,
        and how to give in return."

George Avakian,
a eulogy in the magazine, Jazz

Dolphy's wasn't an easy life…something else was
   more important to him than comfort.
Colleagues remember Eric Dolphy living in poverty
         in a loft in lower Manhattan in 1963, the year
         before his death.

Without heat and with snow blowing
      into the room through cracks in the wall,
            he had nonetheless turned down an offer to
travel again with Mingus, which was a good gig at the time,
               because of Mingus' legendary bad temper.
      {Mingus, on the other hand,
               called Dolphy "a saint."}

      "Eric Dolphy was a saint—
      in every way, not just in his playing." *Charles Mingus*

"Once I saw Eric with an armful of groceries
         and I asked him where he was going. He replied
         that he was on his way to deliver the groceries to
         some musicians who had just gotten into town and
         didn't have anything to eat. I knew he didn't have
         any money (no work) but he did have a $20 gig
         the night before."

                           Richard Davis,
                           bassist on the Eric Dolphy
                           recording of "Come Sunday"

"To me, jazz is like part of living,
         like walking down the street and
         reacting to what you see and hear.
And whatever I do react to,
            I can say immediately in my music."
                     Eric Dolphy,
                     from Eric Dolphy, A Musical Biography and
                     Discography, by Simosko & Tepperman

"This human thing in instrumental playing has to do
with trying to get as much human warmth and feeling
into my work as I can.
I want to say more
on my horn than I ever
could in ordinary speech."

Eric Dolphy

John Coltrane's was a different mix…a different collage,
yet its improvization echoed Dolphy's in spirit.

Born an only child in 1926 in the small town of
Hamlet, North Carolina, Coltrane's family moved
near relatives while he was yet a baby, to the larger
town of High Point. That's where Coltrane grew
up in a middle-class environment, surrounded by
music, education, and religion. His father, a tailor
by trade, played violin and guitar and would relax
alone with his instruments as soon as he returned
home from work, before dinner. This habit
had a powerful impact on his young son. As an
adult, Coltrane was known to practice up to
12 hours a day.

Coltrane's mother served others as a housekeeper and
seamstress. College-educated, she shared her husband's love
of music, singing and playing the piano. Both grandparents
were Methodist ministers.

His maternal grandfather was the most
    influential of all on young Coltrane,
    a real make-it-happen preacher in the community,
    an avid reader and academician.

        At age 10, Coltrane took up the clarinet to
play in a school band…but when he savored the swing-
era hits of Count Basie and the liquid tones of the
Count's saxophonist, Lester Young, Coltrane dropped
his first instrument and picked up an alto saxophone.
He never put it down—practicing whenever and
wherever he could.

Then adversity hit…at age 13,
a few months after discovering the saxophone,
Coltrane lost his father, both of his maternal
grandparents, and his uncle.

    Suddenly his household was without male support and
his mother and aunt took in borders and extra jobs to
make ends meet…the pre-teen became withdrawn, his
school work suffered, and his most consoling friend
and companion became his saxophone.

What had been an enthusiasm became a means of survival;
his saxophone, a spiritual lifeline."

Ashley Kahn,
A Love Supreme:
The Story of John Coltrane's
Signature Album

That lifeline served him well…

    Both Coltrane and Dolphy served in the military
and played in the band—Coltrane in the Navy and
Dolphy in the Army and the U.S. Naval School of Music.

In 1949 Coltrane joined Dizzy Gillespie's big band and stayed with the group until it broke up in May 1950. From 1952 through 1954, he worked with various bands, but a call he received while freelancing in Philadelphia is what propelled him into the public light. The call was from renown trumpeter Miles Davis. Davis was determined to reclaim the popularity he had enjoyed in the 1940s and was forming a quintet. Coltrane became an integral part of the Davis band from 1955 to 1956. The 'Trane had begun to move.

"[Coltrane's] real career spans the twelve years between 1955 and 1967, during which time he reshaped modern jazz and influenced generations of other musicians."

> David Wild,
> *"The Recordings of John
> Coltrane: A Discography"*

But Coltrane was fired from the Davis band in winter of 1956. Excessive drug and alcohol use had taken their toll. Depression followed, and the devastating drug abuse, including heroin, continued.

"Most musicians remain poor. But the music they make, even if it does not bring them millions, gives millions of people happiness."

Langston Hughes

...then, a spiritual awakening took place, as Coltrane later described it.

Several days of intense meditation and prayer brought Coltrane to the clear and distinct decision that he needed to make a change, now. He invited his family's support and stayed in his room for several days, receiving water only when he asked for it. Coltrane emerged a new man, and his re-ignited inner fire only grew brighter with time.

Now the 'Trane couldn't be stopped.

"During the year 1957, I experienced, by
the grace of God, a spiritual awakening
which was to lead me to a richer, fuller,
more productive life. At that time, in
gratitude, I humbly asked to be given the
means and privilege to make others
happy through music."

John Coltrane

"I will do all I can to be worthy of Thee, O Lord.
It all has to do with it.
Thank You God.

"Peace.

"There is none other.
God is. It is so beautiful.

"Thank You God. God is all.

"Help us to resolve our fears and weaknesses

"In you all things are possible.
Thank you God..."

John Coltrane,
from his poem "A Love Supreme"

Trane did a brief gig with Thelonious Monk at
        New York's legendary Five Spot, where more
        than 150 people routinely packed tightly
        together in a small, smoke-filled room to
        soak in the jazz music.
Monk was the headliner, but people soon began to
        appreciate Coltrane as much as Monk.
"Coltrane is so different; he's almost like an
Einstein of music."

> *abstract expressionist painter Willem de Kooning,*
> *who frequented the Five Spot with his friends*

An Einstein of music...Einstein, the one man Coltrane
said he admired more than any other...

Coltrane—ever inquisitive and probing—soon rejoined
with Davis. He exploded with newfound creativity and exploration, developing a way to fill up empty musical spaces, creating
a continuous flow of sound over one chord using different
tones...the critics marveled, calling this new jazz development
"sheets of sound"...some said this discovery paralleled Coltrane's personal search for a greater relationship with God ...
but Coltrane didn't pay attention to the critics... he just kept
playing, seeking, discovering and moving on.

Trane stayed with Davis
through April 1960, finally leaving to follow his
own musical and spiritual exploration more intensely.
He formed a quartet and later made it a quintet by
adding Dolphy, his long time friend.

"For a long time Eric Dolphy and I had
been talking about all kinds of improvising
techniques. Finally, I decided that as long as
my band was working steadily, it made sense
for Eric to join us."   *John Coltrane*

"When you hear
        [live] music, after it's over,
        it's gone in the air.
    You can never capture it again."
                                    Eric Dolphy

"The jazz band is a real creation in novel tonal effects,
whether you like them or not."   *Aaron Copland*

"Whenever I make a change, I'm a little worried that
it may puzzle people. And sometimes I deliberately
delay things for this reason. But after awhile I find
there is nothing else I can do but go ahead."
                                    John Coltrane

"John used to tell me how to listen to the music,
        so that I could get the most out of it.
            He would say things to me like,

'you listen to a song five times, Cecilia.
       Listen to it instrument by instrument.
           Play that song and listen to the bass
               all the way through.
    Listen to it again, and listen to the saxophone.
   Don't just listen to it once and then attempt to give it a
               critique."'

> *Cecilia Foster, cousin of Elvin Jones and*
> *wife of Frank Foster, from Ashley Kahn,*
> *A Love Supreme: The Story of John*
> *Coltrane's Signature Album*

"Sometimes I wish I could walk up to my music
       as if for the first time, as if I had never heard it before.
   Being so inescapably a part of it, I'll never know what
   the listener gets, what the listener feels, and that's too
   bad."   *John Coltrane*

   "Trane's musical approach paralleled my
own development as a sculptor. It was slow and steady,
working out one motif over and over again in a
strongly disciplined manner. He made me realize that
sculpture, which has often been compared to painting,
is really closer to music, because both are three-dimen-
sional art forms expressing fluidity and movement."

> *Bradford Graves*

Enthusists applauded. Critics scorned.

As Coltrane pursued his musical and spiritual searching,
       now with Dolphy in his band,
       some critics said these explorations were
       over-long and avant-garde "anti-jazz" …a criticism
   Coltrane and Dolphy willingly discussed in an interview
           with DownBeat magazine.

Coltrane: "They're [the performances are] long
because all the soloists try to
explore all the avenues that the
tune offers. They try to use all their
resources in their solos. Everybody
has quite a bit to work on…It's not
planned that way; it just happens …
There are times when we play
opposite another group, [when] in
order to play a certain number of
sets a night, you…have to play 45 or
55 minutes [to] rotate sets with the other
band…

But when your set is unlimited timewise, and everything is really together musically…it really doesn't make any
difference how long you play…

If I feel like I'm just playing notes…maybe I don't feel the
rhythm or I'm not in the best shape…I'll try
to build things to the point where this inspiration
is happening again, where things are spontaneous
and not contrived. If it reaches that point again, I
feel it can continue—it's alive again. But if it
doesn't happen, I'll just quit, bow out."

Dolphy: "What I'm trying to do I find enjoyable.…
inspiring—what it makes me do. It helps me
play, this feel…You have an idea [of what
you're going to do next], but there's always
that spontaneous thing that happens. This
feeling, to me, leads the whole group.

When John [Coltrane] plays, it might
lead into something you had no idea could be
done. Or McCoy [Tyner, the pianist] does
something. Or the way Elvin [Jones, the
drummer] or Jimmy [Garrison, the bassist] play;
they solo, they do something in a different way.
I feel that is what [our playing] does for me."

Coltrane, regarding having Dolphy in the band:
"...he came in, and it was like having another
member of the family. He'd found another way
to express the same thing we had found one
way to do...he's had a broadening effect on us.
There are a lot of things we try now that we
never tried before. This helps me..."

"Eric and I have been talking music for quite a
few years, since about 1954. We've been close
for quite a while. We watched music. We always
talked about it, discussed what was being done
down through the years,
because we love music. What we're doing now
was started a few years ago."

*Appreciate the freedom
in the music,
appreciate the freedom and free will
God has given our lives.*

Dolphy died a few years after this interview.

Coltrane wept bitterly. But *his* journey was meant to continue;
    searching and exploring new expressions in music…
    until he died of cancer, just shy of his 41st birthday in
    1967.
        "For all their theoretical sense of freedom, jazz
    musicians have a tendency to be surprisingly
    hidebound [self-limiting]," wrote New York Times
    critic John S. Wilson in 1967. "As a rule, they find
    their mode of expression early in their careers.
    After that… basically the adventure is over." A
    "strong and influential" exception to the rule,
    Wilson quickly noted, was Coltrane's "process of
    constant development."

"In 1960 Coltrane was 33, an age when most of
    his contemporaries sought career stability. Yet his
    most adventurous work—including the creative
    apogee of *A Love Supreme*— was still to come…"

                   Ashley Kahn, "A Love Supreme:
                   The Story of John Coltrane's
                   Signature Album"

A Love Supreme…hailed as Coltrane's masterpiece…
    spilling over in abundant praise to his creator, a song of
    praise incorporating all Trane had learned thus far in
    life…seven years after his life-transforming
    spiritual awakening, several months after the death of
    his dear friend Dolphy…

...now an ordained minister, Coltrane said God revealed
the entire piece *A Love Supreme* in a dream...
From this point on,
Coltrane claims that 90% of his playing is prayer.

Rich fusion of spirituality and
continual musical expression...
but ever human.

Some thought Coltrane was a God...
some people worship great men, great leaders...
some said even the Beatles were more popular than Jesus...
...but do they miss the point?

"Trane and Buddha, both great teachers
in their differing styles and different times, suffered
from similar misconceptions by far too many of their
followers. While alive, they were addressed as gods;
when dead, they were worshipped as God...But I
believe that John William Coltrane was a mystic, a
musician, and a man who changed people's lives,
usually for the better. A reluctant mystic...
a brilliant musician...and a decent man."
J.C. Thomas,
Chasin' the Trane,
The Music and Mystique of John Coltrane

"Coltrane's trademark was his unique sound,
which bespoke a relentless search for perfection
yet was always,
even in the most elevated realms of abstraction,
compellingly passionate and alive."
Nat Hentoff

Life—an ongoing searching ...
discovery...improvisation...
a striving for something higher than oneself...

Two

The Endless Song

He has made everything beautiful in its time.
He has set eternity in the hearts of men;
yet we, with our finite human minds, cannot fathom
what the infinite God,
our loving creator,
has done and will do
from the beginning of the world…and
from the first beat of our hearts…to the end…

In many ways,
music best expresses the mysticism of life…of faith.

The mystery of God is beyondness, the unseen hand
of grace, and music best expresses this mysticism of
life…   *words spoken at a funeral*

It is echoed in the searching culture of the
progressive jazz masters;
in the heart of the passionate athletes;
in the spirit of the cancer victors—
in each soul's journey of faith…

"He [Coltrane] had experimented with various tones,
timbres, fingerings, and even reeds and mouthpieces in order
to find the tone he desired, a tone of feeling, depth and color.
He developed a spontaneous tone full of motion and surprises:

squeaks and hollers, rapid, high-pitched glisses or a switch
characterized by a slow vibrato…Coltrane's music now spoke
of beauty, kindness, God and humanistic values. ."

Emmett G. Price, III,
"The Development of John Coltrane's
Concept of Spirituality and Its Expression in Music"

Indeed,
 "We possess a modicum of life,
   a modicum of truth, and a modicum of love,
   but do we possess them in their entirety?" *Fulton Sheen*

     Ours is not a perfect journey,
      but beautiful nonetheless
    with its unique shades and colors and tones,
    its unique rhythm and quiet pauses…

The soul needs time *and* eternity
 Eternity is a momentary contemplation where time stops;
  Every minute has eternity in it…

 Ah, but we are so rooted in time
    and in human events
      and in human dynamics;
  Yet worldly prizes don't bring happiness,
  and fighting keeps us from the prize…the prize…
        Peace of Mind.

    Live for today…Live for eternity…
     God will take care of the rest…

 We are on a human and spiritual journey,
 full of shortcomings and imperfections…

Life doesn't end
    with a diagnosis of a potentially life-threatening
    disease—for some it truly begins at that moment...

God needs us *as we are*...
    right *now*,
    in the very circumstances we find ourselves...
    ...our spiritual journey...our endless song...

        What are we invited to sing, to play, *today*?

        What instruments can we use today?
            Not "I can't"... but "I can, I *will*"...

        To Whom do we sing?

To be a Christian is to be forever discovering life
    It is not that we blind ourselves to sin and war and
        disease and death,
    but the believer knows the secret that
        in the very midst of death, life exists.

    "The [great] paradox is that by letting go,
  we hold on to the very thing that is permanent:
  not the song, but the source of the song."
            Philip Toshio Sudo
            Zen Guitar

*Praise to God comes naturally
when we count our blessings.*

The source of the song,
>> the endless song, the spiritual journey,
>> the journey of faith...
>> and faith, *pistis* in Greek, meaning
>>> "to believe with assurance and confidence."

How can we believe with assurance and confidence
during what we perceive to be difficult times?

"I can only fly freely
when I know there is a catcher to catch me.
If we are to take risks,
to be free,
in the air,
in life,
we have to know
that when we come down from it all,
we're going to be caught,
we're going to be safe.
The great hero is the least visible.
Trust the catcher."

Henri Nouwen

Wade in the Water

Every faith, every culture,
>> throughout history
>>> has shed light on this journey:

An old Cherokee confided one time to
his young grandson a story about a fight going
on inside himself, a fight between two wolves.

"One wolf is evil," the old man
explained. "Filled with anger, envy, sorrow, regret,
greed, arrogance, self-pity, guilt,
resentment, inferiority, lies, false pride
superiority and ego.

The other wolf is good. He brings joy,
peace, love, hope, serenity, humility, kindness,
benevolence, empathy, generosity, truth,
compassion and faith."

This was very interesting to the young boy.
He quietly thought about it for a
moment, and then asked,

"Which wolf wins, grandfather?"

The wise old Cherokee simply replied,
"The one I feed."

Every faith and culture throughout history has also
respected the mystery of the journey—

One unknown author compares it to
the work of a weaver:

"My life is but a weaving
        between my Lord and me,
        I cannot choose the colors,
        He worketh steadily.

Often times He weaveth sorrow,
        and I in foolish pride
        forget He sees the upper
        and I, the underside.

Not 'til the loom is silent
        and the shuttles cease to fly
        shall God unroll the canvas
        and explain the reason why.

The dark threads are as needful
        in the Weaver's skillful hand
        as threads of gold and silver
        in the pattern He has planned."

Another speaks of the Great Dance:

"All that is made seems planless to the darkened mind,
because there are more plans than it looked for...
        So with the Great Dance.
        "Set your eyes on one movement
        and it will lead you
                through all patterns
        and it will seem to you the master movement.

But the seeming will be true...There seems no plan
　　because it is all plan:
　　　there seems no centre because it is all centre.
Blessed be he!"

C.S. Lewis, "Voyage to Venus"

...and all along our journey,
　　cancer victors encourage us to:

　　　Bless each day.
　　　Sanctify the moment. Follow our hearts...
　　　　be thankful for all we do have...

　　　"Our hearts were made for Thee,
　and they are restless until they rest in Thee, O Lord."

St. Augustine

　"...we do not and cannot know when the
world drama will end. The curtain may be rung
down at any moment: say, before you have finished
reading this paragraph...
　　We do not even know whether we are in Act 1
or Act V. We do not know who are the major and
who the minor characters. The Author knows.

　The audience, if there is an audience (if angels and
archangels and all the company of heaven fill the pit
and the stalls), may have an inkling.

　But we, never seeing the play from outside,
　　never meeting any characters except the tiny minority
　　who are "on" in the same scenes as ourselves,
　　wholly ignorant of the future and
　　very imperfectly informed about the past,
cannot tell at what moment the end ought to come.

That it [the end] will come when it ought,
we may be sure; but we waste our time in guessing
when that will be. That it has a meaning we may be sure, but
we cannot see it.

When it is over, we may be told. We are led to
expect that the Author will have something to say to
each of us on the part that each of us has played.
The playing it well is what matters infinitely."

C.S. Lewis, "Fern-seed and Elephants"

"This is not our home...We have something in our hearts
which nothing in this world can satisfy."

Fulton Sheen

Life...a gift beyond measure,
    an endless song,
        a continuum of aspiration and conversion;

a journey—
        filled with improvisation as well as structure
            and guideposts.

Not perfect...
        never completely finished...

Three

Be Not Afraid

When you feel fear or loneliness...
>>you are not alone, dear reader,

Imagine the most loving smiles you've ever seen on
your closest friends, family and relatives, and
even other faces throughout your life...

Imagine these people clearly and distinctly, the
most loving people in your life...

Now imagine what it would be like to be in a
room *only with these most loving people.*

>>>What would it feel like?

>>>Would you feel immersed in tenderness,
>>>>love and affection?

>>>Would you want to share that feeling
>>>>with others?

>>>Would you too have a radiant,
>>>>heartfelt smile
>>>>>on your lips?
>>>>>>in your heart?

Now look just over the shoulders of all the people in
this room... See a person standing behind all of them
who is even more loving than each of these people... He is
looking at you, through the loving eyes of all of
>>these other people. The face of Christ...

The love we have in this world is
only a pretaste of God's
great and merciful love.
Why do we have to be reminded to be not afraid...
especially when we are surrounded by so much beauty,
love and enjoyment—
so many things that point to our eternal home?

A cancer victor, a young breast cancer patient,
chose to live this truth.
She lived it in a beautiful, simple way:

News of her final return to the hospital
was followed by her request for a visit.

It's only human... No matter who you are, it can be
a little tough to respond eagerly when asked to visit
someone near death...even if you only
know them casually or professionally...

But you do it anyway,
because you know it could be
comforting for them,
or for their family or friends...

Still, you don't know how you'll be greeted—
Will they be in pain? crying? in fear?
sadness or anger? sleeping?
Will they be weak, sapped of all strength,
alone or with friends?
Will they need comfort?
What words should be said?
What would it be like to see her?

I knocked and opened the door:
She was sitting up, on the edge of the bed,
Pale, but alert and smiling...

Her smile lit up the room,
That smile continued throughout our entire visit...
    she knew it was a matter of hours or days—
And the phrase she'd heard before,
                so many times...
                in healthy times,
                in recovery times,
    She spoke now with confidence and assurance.

There was a certain majesty in her tone of voice,
    a certain hope and lovingness in her eyes,
        hard to capture in words—
        the impression was that she
        wore the unseen crown of a victor...

    "You know what I'm going to say...
                    be not afraid."
    "I knew you were going to say that,
                I'm not afraid."

A rush of inspiration,
    like the exhilaration one feels when a
            marching band plays...
    unspoken,
    but very real. very powerful.
    Inspiration of a lifetime—
            words that came to life,
            that were lived,
    even to the end of this patient's life the next day :
                    Be not afraid.

Victors of faith do not live in fear.

Yes, unfortunately, some people
        suffer mental anguish and physical suffering.

        But can we find meaning in this?
        Is there any human comparison?

In Roman times, the cruelest and most punishing death
                          was death on a cross...
        left to starve, left to struggle for air,
            left for others to mock publicly...

        and before that death, in a garden not far away,
listen to the cry of an innocent:

"Father, if thou wilt, remove this chalice from me:
        but not my will, but thine be done.
And there appeared to him an angel from heaven,
        strengthening him.
        And being in an agony, he prayed the longer..."
                                        Luke 22: 42-44

Some people offer up the pain, the fear...for others...

        Imagine the stories of innocent prisoners who nobly
        gave their life for friend or family...
            Consider the most innocent
            prisoner who gave his life to all mankind...

                    There is no greater love.

Not
"Better them than me,"
            but rather,
                "Better me than them."

Thank God for Hospice and for pain management specialists,
        whose goals include keeping us pain-free
        and clear-headed, with dignity.

"Letting go of ambitions will let go of anxiety,
        Don't need to wallow, but care,
                        a soft activity..."
                                        Thomas More

"God is at the heart of every person's present moment."
Bishop Henry Mansell

"Peace I leave with you.
My peace I give to you."
John 14:27

Have you heard?
There is Good News:
    death has been conquered,
    and Victors of Faith have only to focus on
        Living to the end and giving to the end...

"Let not your heart be troubled, ye believe in God,
believe also in me...I go to prepare a place for you.
And if I go and prepare a place for you,
I will come again and receive you unto myself.
That where I am, there ye may be also..."
John 14:1-3

There is other good news...
    The majority of all patients diagnosed with cancer
        today are cured with proper treatment...
    Some of the earliest forms of cancer have cure rates
        approaching 99 to 100%...

Good news?

Bad news?

God knows.

Like the angels in the Bible
     even when bearing good news,
     we, too, must preface our announcements of good
     news with:
              "Be not afraid."

Come fear and death no longer...
          rather,
              Come Sunday.

Four

Bearing the Cross of Uncertainty

Have you ever considered how much we take for granted?

We expect the car to start when we turn the ignition key,
a dial tone to be heard when we pick up the phone,
a day at school or work to begin as usual,
a seed to turn into a plant...

But the truth is,
Life has its uncertainties.

Little things can get in the way,
Circumstances can change dramatically,
Unforeseen opportunities can arise.

The story line of your life's book may change,
but when God is the author, happiness will ultimately prevail.

Cancer victors know this
Jazz legends know this
Great coaches know this...

Cancer victors live with a sense of uncertainty about
their disease—
They face routine follow-up tests
to determine whether their disease has recurred.

While some people live in almost constant anticipation
of their next test,
the victors accept this reality,
      and turn it into a life-positive experience.

Even though a patient may have a highly curable cancer
due to early diagnosis, each patient lives through his or
her follow-up in different ways...

      The impact of reality...a new sharp, clear
      perspective about what's important in life—and
      what isn't. Victors recognize in that newfound
      perspective an intense gift of life...
           of opportunity.

For example,
      If an early cancer has a 99% cure rate, does a
      patient choose to live in fear of being in the 1%
      that fail?

      If a cancer has a 50% cure rate, does a patient
      approach life as though he or she is in the 50%
      that won't survive, or in the 50% that will?

      What if the cancer has a 1% cure rate and a
      99% failure rate...

Remember, you are not alone...
      As one great jazz musician put
      it, "We don't like to think about
      it...but we all gotta go."

Trumpeter Al Hirt and clarinetist Pete Fountain are
legendary jazz musicians of New Orleans.

As a special tribute to New Orleans when it hosted Super Bowl
IX, Hirt and Fountain recorded Super Jazz I, capturing the

rich New Orleans jazz culture and enhancing the Super Bowl festivities.

> In this recording, Al Hirt talks about a long-standing New Orleans jazz tradition:

> "When one of the [band] members dies,
> the band will go out and play.
> They will play one of those old hymns
> and they will play it two ways.

>> First of all, they will play it softly and sadly, you know, a dirge and a funeral march, on the way to the cemetery, the gravesite.

>> When they get there, they feel the spirit now has gone on to a greater reward and it's time for happiness, so they play it in a jazz tempo...

> ...We don't like to think about it,
> but we all gotta go, right?

> You know, I talked to the boys and said
> 'Look, I want me one of those jazz funerals,'
> and they told me, they said, 'Jumbo, you in the book.'

>> I'm in the book. 'Fountain's in the book.
>> Pee Wee's in the book. You can play at
>> mine and I'll play at yours.'"
>>> *Al Hirt,*
>>> *Super Jazz I*

That's just it.

> There are statistics that reveal a small but definite risk that a 50- to 60-year-old, even a younger person,

who shows no symptoms,
    may die within the next 20 minutes.
        The next 20 minutes…

  Everyone worries about a patient with a life-threatening
diagnosis, even if the risk is over a
        20-year period or longer.

            But how many times have other,
            seemingly healthy people gone first?

    There's no such thing as zero risk.

    There's no such thing as a 50% cure either.
      We'll either survive the disease or we won't.

    After receiving the best treatments and follow-up care,
    a patient may have no more control over whether their
            disease will recur or not…

But cancer victors choose to live like they will survive—
    They opt to play right through it.
    They live to the end and give to the end,
            with no regrets.

Is this so different from the young soldier in harm's way?
Or the innocent citizen living in an uncertain world?

    Yes, we may live in times of serious fears—
        but we can still find happiness …

Jazz musicians play from the heart,
    each performance a new mix of raw spontaneity and
    well-rehearsed phrases.
    But even the best musician isn't always on a roll—
      sometimes it's there, and sometimes it's not.

What happens on stage is uncertain, on edge, alive ...

"You have this idea of what you're going to do
next, but there's always that spontaneous thing
that happens..."

Eric Dolphy

"If I feel like I'm just playing notes...
maybe I don't feel the rhythm or I'm not in
the best shape... I'll try to build
things to the point where this
inspiration is happening again, where things are
spontaneous and not contrived. If it reaches
that point again, I feel it can continue—it's alive
again. But if it doesn't happen, I'll just
quit, bow out."

John Coltrane

"Grab your coat and get your hat.
Leave your worries at the doorstep.
Just direct your feet
To the sunny side of the street."

"On the Sunny Side of the Street"
Dorothy Fields and Jimmy McHugh, 1929

Coaches, too, know that their career could depend on winning
or losing games—
>They know the power of motivation, focus,
>preparation and heart...
>They also know they don't have total control over
>>what happens on the field or on the court on
>>>game day...

Uncertainty,
>not what one person must bear alone...
>no, not at *all.*

>Uncertainty is a part of every day life;
>we *all* must bear a cross of uncertainty...

Some people imagine a small cross or bag over their shoulder,
>they imagine it contains all their worries or uncertainties,
>>it helps them keep their anxieties in perspective
>>and allows them to get on with their lives.

We are not alone.
>No one has to bear their burdens alone.
>Victors of faith feel comforted that there is always
>>Someone there to help them bear
>>their burden of uncertainty.

Yes, uncertainty is an integral part of life,
>but the victors show us another option for living—

>Not whimpering or complaining,
>not wringing hands or worrying,
>not anxious,
>not paralyzed in fear...
>>...but living fully
>>>in hope,
>>>in love,
>>>>in the simplicity and reality
>>>>of the present moment.

Patients with cancer often challenge us:
  can worrying add one iota to our stature?
  can it change the future?
  can it change *anything at all?*

  Instead,
      worrying can make us miserable,
        distract us from what is real, here and now,
          from joy or pain or sorrow or love...

We, too, can become like these cancer victors
    even amid uncertain times,
        uncertain outcomes or
        uncertain situations...

They bear the cross of uncertainty with
                      dignity and grace...
                      inner calm,
                      self-abandonment...

    and in this way,
        they do not squander or waste the
        present moment they've been given.

NFL Hall of Fame coach Marv Levy led the Buffalo Bills to
    four straight Super Bowls. As his players huddled
    around him at the start of each game,
    his famous charge was:

  "Where would you rather be than right here, right now?"

        How did a great coach like Marv Levy deal
    with uncertainty and potential anxiety during the week
    before a professional football game,
                and in his personal life?

Coach Levy discussed this with me for the readers of this book:
"I didn't experience pregame anxiety as an NFL coach,
        I didn't experience anxiety and here's why. I always
        preached to my players that if you prepare well, the
        night before the game is the easiest night of the
        week. The key is to prepare well."

Applying his philosophy to life, he continued:

"The key is to prepare well, and to gain understanding
        and perspective about your opponent or about a
        situation. If things don't turn out as you planned, you
        go back and do it again, only this time you do it
        for the new situation: re-prepare, re-understand
        and gain new perspective.

        I won't tell you that I block out bad circumstances or
        somehow rise above them. I don't. No one does. No
        matter how an athlete or coach's face looks to
        the public eye, no one blocks it out. You go
        through the fire like everyone else, on
        and off the playing field. As a coach, you do
        your homework. You're prepared for your opponent.
        You get focused on what you have to do and don't get
        fretful over the distractions.

        That goes for anything in life. You have to ride out the
        challenges, the obstacles and the circumstances that
        come your way. Worry adds nothing.

I'll give you a personal example.
        A few years ago, my diagnosis of prostate cancer took
        me by surprise. I'm used to being prepared and this
        blew me away. Yes, I felt confused and overwhelmed at
        first. Who wouldn't? But you have to move beyond that.

Right away I started poring over articles and books. You have
to learn as much as you can and gain an understanding of it.

That helped tremendously. Then you have to play it out. You
do what you have to do, and you do it with an inner
confidence that you've prepared as best you could. You
move forward.

The night before surgery I can honestly say that I did
not want to be right there, right then. The uncertainty
was there. Gratefully, my outcome was excellent.

I've seen this kind of thing again and again.
I've seen great players face tough times.
I've seen a few real devastating situations.
But always, after the initial period of maybe confusion or shock,
     always you get back on your feet,
          get prepared and face the challenge head-on
                    with confidence.

     Take Chris Spielman, the All-American football player
at Ohio State who went on to become one of the great
All-Pro NFL players. He suffered an injury on the field that
shortened his career.

          To cut short that kind of football career was
          devastating. But you know what? Devastating as
          this was, his wife was diagnosed with
          breast cancer soon after that.

          Chris quickly gained new perspective. He was
right there to support his wife. He even shaved his head to
show his support when the chemotherapy caused her to lose
her hair. Later on, he joined her in the public campaign against
breast cancer. It was the right thing to do and he did it.

     I'm not saying it was easy, none of it was.
     But he saw what he had to do and he did it.
     He walked through the fire with confidence.

There's no time to waste in this life on anxiety or worry.
  Life isn't certain. It's always changing, it's fluid.
  When change comes, you have to focus on preparation,
  understanding and gaining perspective.
  That's absolutely true!
  The key is to prepare well."

Marv Levy,
Hall of Fame NFL coach

But preparation and perspective
            are not always easy for consummate worriers...

      Take the case of one big-hearted grandmother who
              over the years dutifully earned the reputation of
              doing all the worrying for the family...

      Oh, the whining and worrying
              about a biopsy for a very low suspicion lesion
              that was clearly either benign or an early and
              easily treatable tumor...

      Nothing could calm her.

Finally I smiled and said to her,
        "Let's make a deal—
        You must have a lot of other things that deserve your
        worry much more than this, don't you?"

      She agreed...and began listing those worries.
      Her family all nodded and grinned in agreement,
      "*Oh boy*, does she have a lot of things to worry about!"

I continued:
"You don't worry about this biopsy. Let us worry about that.
And you worry about all those other important things, OK?"
Suddenly this wonderful grandmother stopped talking.
She looked up at me and smiled—

a genuine smile from the heart.
     She was a trooper par excellence,
          something her sons and daughters knew well.

As the husband of one patient with cancer stated:

> "We've been through so much in our lives, some real
> tragedy, that we decided not to waste our energy
> worrying about what hasn't happened yet or what may
> never come to pass."

Yes, the story line of your life's book may change,
but when God is the author, happiness will ultimately prevail—
               Come Sunday,
                    Come Sunday...

Five

Coping with Tragedy

Catastrophic tragedy.
So great a personal loss, that the mind and heart can
barely take it in.

We go into shock....
and that shock seems like a gift.

An emotional holocaust...a raging thunderstorm of
different feelings...seething, churning, pounding...
vomiting, unable to sleep, crying, crying...
when will it end?
when will the sun shine again?
when will the dark night pass?

a reprieve...
then another wave rolls in...

...muscles are tense and twitch in spasm...
twenty voices inside your head...twenty images
flash before your eyes, spurred on by a single
image, a single memory ...it all floods
back...your insides,
like a shipwreck...

But there are some to comfort us—
those who are more seasoned,
wiser than we,
who have lived longer lives,
who have experienced other tragedies,

In their eyes you see great tenderness,
    they are confident that a peaceful morning will come,
                even for us...

    They live the pain,
        but they tell us to let go
        to let God be in control,
        to simplify,
            to be humble,
                to be still and quiet,

        They tell us it's OK to seek help...
           it's OK to shut down a bit,
        to take a break,
            just let our hair grow,
            ignore the things that aren't
            really necessary...

    "Ride out the storm," they say.
    Ride out the storm.
    This too shall pass.

Thank God,
    these tragedies aren't an every day occurrence...

Thank God,
    there is a way to keep perspective.
        Even amid the turmoil of emotions,
        our inner dialog can be calmed...

Connect, find consolation with friends or family ...

    If you are among those giving comfort,
    even offering 1% of yourself and prayer can help...
        to just be there, to listen,
        to hold a hand, touch a shoulder,
        give a hug...

"I am with you all days,
even to the
consummation of the world."

Matthew 28:20

"Peace I leave with you,
My peace I give unto you:

not as the world giveth
do I give unto you.

Let not your heart be troubled,
nor let it be afraid."

John 14:27

"Time heals what reason cannot."

Seneca, Agamemnon
Roman playwright,
philosopher, and politician
{5 BC-65 AD}

"Great time makes all things dim."

Sophocles, Ajax
Greek playright
{496 BC-406 BC}

Yes, time heals.
It heals even big wounds...

But love,
Love is the greatest Healer...

Love laid down His life for his friends,
friends who didn't fully appreciate it...

Even to be a comfort to another person,
    is to lay down your life
        in some way…

    How beautiful an offering of self,
        to dedicate all or even a small part
        of your future for a friend,
        to offer up your sorrow for a friend,
    it's the greatest act of love.

God loves you.
God has a plan for you,
        for each one of us,
        for all peoples…

    He is, ultimately,
        the God of happiness…

No matter how things appear on the surface,
    sad events and tragedies affect everyone in this life—
    strangers, friends, even the famous…

    and somehow, in a monumental tragedy,
        even strangers can feel like friends,
            even if we see only their faces on the
            evening news,
        and share their sorrow, their pain.

Such a moment resonates in us
    perhaps because it renews in our hearts
        all the passions and losses we have suffered,
    or those that have been suffered throughout history—
        by men and women of bygone ages
        on whose shoulders we stand today…

perhaps it calls to mind the profound passion of Christ,
who sweat blood in a garden,
for the sake of true love,
for the sake of friends
who didn't fully understand at the time...

Yes, tragedy compels us to stop and listen,
brings us together,
connects us in ways we couldn't have imagined,
in the immediacy of "now,"
a great timeless Passion...

Both in your sorrow
and in your soaring,
there is a parallel—
both are aspirations that lead to something higher,
something more beautiful,
Someone more loving...
God

It is He who tenderly draws us to himself in these moments...

Suffering can be endured painfully.
Suffering can be accepted as bearing a cross.
Suffering can also be given
the meaning and purpose of a cross.

Cancer victors are victors of faith...
They tell us there's no need to worry,
their very lives proclaim
that He cannot fail to bring us Easter Sunday
after Good Friday...

These victors of faith bring quiet perspective to the moment,
they show us how to calm our inner dialogues...

And is there not a special peace
and contentment
in the eyes of those victors who have endured suffering—
unspoken...but real?

And again, when we face monumental tragedies—
as a nation, as a family, as a group of friends,
as an individual—

Like the pine seed that opens during the forest fire,
tragedy opens our hearts to become more human,
more loving,
more connected to the moment,
to God, to eternity...
to Sunday.

Thank God,
tragedy isn't all there is,
in spite of its initial gripping impact...

"God whispers to us in our pleasures,
speaks to us in our conscience,
but shouts in our pains:
it is his megaphone to rouse a deaf world."
C.S. Lewis, The Problem of Pain

Michael Flynn is a cancer institute administrator.
His insights on how to cope with tragedy are personal
and heartfelt...

Here is an excerpt from Mr. Flynn's talk,
   given at an annual remembrance service for cancer
   patients' families,
            but it is not a talk about cancer...

"Tonight is a special night because for many in attendance
               it is the first time they have returned
               since the death of a loved one...
I would like to share with you some thoughts
      on the forces that I believe allowed you to come,
            what I call
                  the courage to remember,
                  the determination not to forget.

When asked to be part of tonight's service,...
      I was agreeing to share some of my most personal
            experiences with a group of strangers...
      I was forcing myself to come face-to-face with the dark
            memories we all carry with us after a loss...
      I needed to overcome the reluctance to speak about an
            event in my life that undeniably altered
            my views on the everyday existence
                  we sometimes take so casually.
      I needed to find the courage and determination
            to once again find the courage to remember,
            the determination not to forget.

...I came to understand that courage was
      an uncommon characteristic of common men and
      women, displayed under conditions that should
      never have to be experienced, certainly never repeated.
            Determination was the supporter when courage
            maybe waned a bit.

Brian Flynn is my son,…the first of four children. …
Brian was the one from whom
    I learned about parenting, about growing up, about
    caring for another in a special way…about uncondi-
    tional love, giving and receiving. He grew to be my best
    friend.

And then, in one instant,
        from one phone call,
            lives changed.

    Brian was 17, just two months shy of his 18th
birthday and 11 days into his career as a student at West
Virginia University. On the evening of Monday, August
28, 1989, we spoke with Brian and he stated he was not
feeling well, suffering from some headaches. He stated
he had experienced a fairly active second weekend at
college, some parties, some tennis, and little sleep. He
had also complained the week before of the food and
had not necessarily been eating well. He said he was going to get some sleep for he had class the next morning.
We said good-bye and that we would call him Tuesday
evening to see how he was feeling.

    On Tuesday, August 29, we returned from a dinner
with friends and immediately called Brian's dorm room.
The time of the call was 9:16 p.m., as painfully noted
on the long distance bill we received the following
month. A strange voice answered the phone, and when
asked his name, he identified himself as the Resident
Advisor (RA) and asked who I was. I identified myself
as Brian's father. The RA stated he had just found Brian
and that he was being rushed to the hospital.

    About 75 minutes later our phone rang. The voice
identified itself as the head of the Department of
Neurosurgery at Ruby Memorial Hospital, the teaching

hospital located on the campus of WVU. After a few disclaimers about 'we are not sure what happened, but no drugs or alcohol are suspected,' the doctor proceeded to tell me that all indications were that Brian was 'brain dead,' and we should make plans to come to Morgantown.

We left immediately, driving five hours in the middle of the night, leaving behind all semblance of a 'normal' life, entering the blackness of initial bereavement due to the loss of a child.

After a day of mandatory testing, at 5 p.m., on August 30, the attending neurologist told us he had declared Brian dead. He tried to explain what had happened, stating the rarity of the condition and how he found it unbelievable that there were no manifestations of this condition prior to the day before. But none of this changed a thing... Brian was waked over the 1989 Labor Day weekend and was buried on September 5.

In the days and weeks following Brian's death,
    I realized that a conscious decision needed to be made.
    I could accept what had happened,
        and live the remainder of my life in the grip of
        Sorrow.

Or, I could confront that demon, Sorrow, head on,
    and someday, after winning more of the daily
    battles than I lost, I could live the 'new normal'
    that is our lives after we lose someone special to us.

But I had to come to terms with the amount of
    courage and determination that would take.

Because I knew I would never forget that Brian died,
>I needed to find the courage and determination
>to always remember that Brian lived!

So I set out on a quest.
>A quest to beat back those demons.
>I attended meetings of The Compassionate Friends,
>a support group for parents who have lost children.
>The first time we drove to the church where the meeting
>was held, we sat in the car wondering what to do next.
>There was no way we could walk into a room of strangers
>>all gathered to discuss their feelings
>>since their child died…

But we summoned our courage and determination,
>walking slowly, quietly, into a room full of
>parents who had all experienced what we were feeling.

>In a few short minutes, we were sharing our story
>>with a group of strangers,
>>all of whom became friends and supporters…

In his song *The Dance*, Garth Brooks tells of a love lost,
>one that perhaps might have been better never experienced:

>'Our lives are better left to chance,
>>I could have missed the pain but I'd have had to
>>>miss the dance.'

I have learned that it takes courage and determination
>to make the minutes turn into hours,
>>then into days,
>>>into weeks and then into years.

It takes courage and determination to go from
>counting the days since you last saw your loved one,
>>to counting weeks, then months,

and finally, using generalities,
    you reach a point where you tell questioners
    that your son died a little over 12 years ago.

It takes courage and determination to work your way to
    a point where the pain dulls,
        though ever present, and
    it takes courage and determination
to allow the memories of what was to become brighter…
to share with others the story of a life ended much,
    much too soon…
to smile again, laugh again, and sometimes, to love again.

The courage and determination to become 'normal' again,
    within a sorely changed context,
        can conquer that visitor, Sorrow.

    It won't permanently leave,
        but becomes a less frequent visitor.

Courage and determination will allow the smiles to return,
    will let the sunshine brighten the soul again,
    will give you the time to heal…
    'missing the dance' would not have been the answer…

    My prayer for you is that you may always find
    the courage and determination to remember!"
        Michael Flynn,
        cancer institute administrator

Will the pain ever go away?
    In some ways, no, you can't erase it… but it *will* change
        it *will* get better…
    You can calm the
        raging fire
    into a
        small burning ember—

Like a burning ember,
      buried and sometimes hidden,
         yet always there,
ready to flare up and pierce the heart anew...
      yet
         like an endless flame of love,
           a flame of love that stays in the heart...

      an eternal flame that remembers...

"We could not learn to be brave and patient
           if there were only joy in the world."
                Helen Keller

When I listen to the rolling thunder
      of an approaching storm,
God seems so great,
      and I feel so small.

         Come apart and rest awhile,
         or you may just plain come apart.
           Harner

     Sickness and death,
        a time for stoic humility, nothingness...
     This too shall pass,
        wait several moons.   *Anonymous*

"Take up your cross
      and follow Me..."   *Imitation of Christ*

Amazing Grace

"The best thing about the future is
that it only comes one day at a time."

Abraham Lincoln

Your saving, healing ship
of love and grace
will come ...

John Newton was born in London in 1725,
and became the most unlikely person to have
eventually penned the popular hymn *Amazing Grace*—

His mother died when he was yet a child.
His father was commander of a merchant ship that
sailed in the Mediterranean ...

John had received some religious instruction from his mother,
but as a young adult he'd long abandoned any
semblence of faith...

He was only eleven years old when he first went to sea.
After six voyages together, his father retired.
At age 19,
John was pressed into service on a man-of-war,
the H.M.S. Harwich...
conditions were intolerable
and he deserted.

Recaptured and publicly flogged,
he was demoted from midshipman to
common seaman...
and his nightmare worsened...

Finally,
>> John requested, and received, transfer
>> to serve on a slave ship,
>>> the servant of a slave trader...
> he was brutally abused.

An old friend of his father's rescued him.
> John was 23 years old.

John Newton then captained his own ship,
>> a slave trading ship.
But in May of that year, not long after his rescue,
>> a violent storm
> —a storm so bad that John fully expected to perish—
>> completely changed his life...

An avid journal-keeper,
> John documented his voyages, observations and
> experiences...

His journal reveals that it was while
>> trying to steer his ship through the violent storm
>> that he experienced what he later described as
>> his "great deliverance."

He wrote that when all seemed lost
>> and it seemed certain the ship would sink,
>> he cried out,
>>> "Lord, have mercy upon us."

Later in his cabin, he reflected on what he had said...
it became clear to him that God had addressed him
through the storm,
and that grace had begun to work in his life
at that moment...

He went on marry, to educate himself in Latin, Greek
and Hebrew, and many other subjects, including
Holy Scripture.

Although at first rejected in his request to become a minister
in the Church of England,
he persisted.
Eventually he was ordained,
becoming a most popular and powerful
minister, and writing a prodigious amount of
hymns, many of which appear in
Olney Hymns...
But for the rest of his life,
John observed May 10, 1748, as the day of his
conversion, a day of humiliation in which he
subjected his will to a higher power.

from Amazing Grace:
The Story of John Newton, by Al Rogers

Thro' many dangers, toils and snares,
I have already come;
'Tis grace has brought me safe thus far,
And grace will lead me home.

Amazing Grace
John Newton, 1779

"Amazing grace! (how sweet the sound)
    That sav'd a wretch like me!
I once was lost, but now am found,
    Was blind, but now I see.

'Twas grace that taught my heart to fear,
    And grace my fears reliev'd;
How precious did that grace appear,
    The hour I first believ'd!

Thro' many dangers, toils and snares,
    I have already come;
'Tis grace has brought me safe thus far,
    And grace will lead me home.

The Lord has promis'd good to me,
    His word my hope secures;
He will my shield and portion be,
    As long as life endures.

Yes, when this flesh and heart shall fail,
    And mortal life shall cease;
I shall possess, within the veil,
    A life of joy and peace.

The earth shall soon dissolve like snow,
    The sun forbear to shine;
But God, who call'd me here below,
    Will be forever mine."

John Newton

Stay the course,
    your saving ship will come...

    the morning sun will rise
        on a new day and a new era...

    We're all human,
    don't get down on yourself...

        It's OK to take the needed break,
        just like some of the great actors, athletes and
        coaches do—
            after a demanding movie production
                schedule or season ends,
          they shun the public eye for a bit,
            regain inner strength,
            regroup,
                relax and be still...

It's OK...
    to let go and let God...

    Like the flowers that bloom after the rain...
        and sometimes it rains so hard
    that it seems the flowers will not survive...

    but they do.
    And you will too,
        more beautiful,
        more radiant,
        more peaceful
            than ever you could imagine...

            Come Sunday...

Six

Inspiration for a Lifetime

Sometimes people wonder
    whether a person can
        have much influence
on the world
        if they are
            sick,
            or old,
    or suffering,
            or confined to a room...

On the surface it may seem that
        they don't make much of an impact,

            but that is only a shallow impression...

Have you noticed that beautiful and majestic trees
                                come to life
            where hidden seeds are planted?

How many great doctors,
                musicians, actors,
                artisans, teachers,
                mothers, fathers,
                pastors,
                        and so many others
            were inspired to do what they do today
        because of the inspiring example of a sick or
            confined relative, friend,
                    colleague or stranger they
                    encountered?

At the time,
    that inspiration seemed little—
        too small to be measured,
        forgotten amid seemingly bigger concerns,
        not worth much...

But today,
    that same quiet, hidden inspiration may have grown into a
        mighty oak, a healthy and fruitful plant...

    What was not visible on the surface,
    was yet planted in the secret recesses of the heart—
        perhaps in the heart of a young person,
        or of a mother or a father who faced struggles
            at the time...

    Much later that tiny seed matured and
        brought life and inspiration to so many others
            through the years...

    Who could have imagined such a powerful impact
        from inspiration so short,
            so humble,
            so subtle at times?

Many great men and women today tell us that
    the simplest of persons or situations in their lives
    has proven to be inspiration for a lifetime beyond
            themselves...

    One colleague, a leading leukemia doctor,
        is candid in telling any who ask
    that he lost his father at a young age to cancer...
    Did his father influence his entire life?
    He sure did!

A young medical student
> points to her father's enduring love
> and belief in her abilities,
>> even as she witnessed his
>> living and giving to the end,
>>> right up to his final days .
> Her father's attitude, even in his final illness,
>> inspired her lifetime decision to help other
>>> patients with cancer.

Another doctor
> recalls how the seed to help patients in cancer centers
> was planted in fifth grade—

>> It was a time when he accompanied
>> his mother and grandmother to a cancer center
>> for treatment of his grandmother's advanced
>>> breast cancer...

> Did this boy know that he wanted to be a doctor?
>> Not at all.

> A seed of inspiration was planted,
> even in the way his grandmother
>> spoke to his mother at the time of his
>> grandmother's death.
> That day his exhausted mother
>> came home a changed and refreshed person.
>> Circumstances were the same,
>> but her attitude was
>>> very changed and different...

With nurturing and encouragement,
> that seed of inspiration,
>> grew,
> as it has in the lives of so many others.

What a privilege,
that you or I could be an inspiration to another,
without even knowing it...

Educators appreciate this...

"The two great goals of education are
to help young people grow both academically
and as people of good character.

It is a tremendous privilege and responsibility
to inspire young people
to develop the strength
of character and faith
that will positively shape
the next generation."

Richard Parisi,
Principal of an elementary school in
Liverpool, NY, that was recognized as a
National School of Character

Powerful intertwining of life experiences...
teaching and learning...giving and receiving...
even without words...
a caring spirit,
a listening heart,
a soothing way...

An attitude toward life that
plays right through the challenges,
embraces the sufferings,
and yet still chooses to muster a smile,
a kind word,
an understanding glance
for others.

Cancer victors gently teach us about the responsibility of the
faithful as they approach the end of their earthly
lives—to live with no regrets,
   to recognize that the greatest gift they can leave
         behind is to give faith and hope to
               future generations...

"He that lives in hope,
     dances without music."
                    George Herbert

         Cancer victors
             have said to their doctors:

"Doctor...I appreciate what you have done for me
     with your medicine and science,
     but I hope that you too
             will take the time in your life
             to enjoy all the blessings
             I have had in mine."

Indeed, some people leave inspiration for a lifetime,
                    others for many lifetimes...

         "Niko" means victory in Greek,
         and is stamped upon the leavened bread
         used in the Divine Liturgy of the
         Byzantine church—
                    the Ultimate Victory,
                         the Ultimate Inspiration.

"Jesus had to leave
     to make room for the Holy Spirit in each of us…"
                                        Fr. Benedict Groeschel

Victors of Faith do not walk around prominently displaying
          their faith on their shoulder or in their speech,
          but nonetheless live life
                    with a faith stamped securely in their
                                        hearts.

They enjoy each day the Lord has given.

"I knew by the smoke that so gracefully curled
          above the green elms that a cottage was near
And I said, "If there's peace to be found in the world
          A heart that was humble might hope for it here."
                              from "Ballad Stanzas," by
                              Irish poet Thomas Moore,
                              inspired by his visit to
                              Batavia, New York, in 1804.

"God has given different gifts to different people.
There is no basis for feeling inferior to another
          who has received a different gift—

Once it is realized that we will be judged
          by the gift we have received,
          rather than by the gift we have not,
          one is completely delivered from a sense of
                              false inferiority…"
                                        Fulton Sheen

"God enters by a private door into every individual."
                                        Ralph Waldo Emerson

"The influence of individual character
    extends from generation to generation."

Iain Macleod

"The love we have known
    in the life of someone who has died
    can be carried on in our own life.
It is this love
    that makes our difficult farewells endurable
        and our grief consolable."

Joyce Rupp

Do you wish to be the salt of the earth?
    Just as many salt particles change and season food,
    So also Victors of Faith are charged with the
    responsibility to change the world...
        at least their little portion of the world...
            They see their time on earth as a
                function of eternity...

Bloom where you are planted...

"Make heroic verse out of the prose of each day."

Josemaria Escriva de Balaguer

"Our highest happiness consists
in the feeling that another's good is purchased by our sacrifice."

Fulton Sheen

"Spiritual kindness is offering people acceptance
    as well as a little of our time and attention
        when they are with us,
            no matter what their response may be."

Robert Wichs

Like a tiny seed carried far and wide by the wind,
   who knows where it will fall,
   or in what soil it will take root and grow...
         will it be in the heart of a spouse,
                  a friend,
                  a colleague,
                        a parent,
         a son or daughter, grandchild,
         cousin, niece or nephew...

Perhaps it will quietly fall into the heart of an
observant stranger,
      and become inspiration for a lifetime...

Seven

Live to the End, Give to the End

Life is for the living—
  each moment,
 a wonderful gift,
  a new opportunity
   filled with unique possibilities,
    with possibilities of giving
     that fit each unique personality,
      and each unique circumstance...

At what moment will our earthly journey end?
  No man or woman knows the answer...
      Only God knows...

But no matter where you are along the journey,
      each day,
        each moment
       is new,

   and it's never too late to begin *now*
     or to begin anew,
    to live with heart and faith—

"Let us begin now,
  because before now we have done nothing."
        St. Francis of Assisi
        on the last day of his life

Like a marathon runner—
    not sprinting as fast as he can,
       but pacing himself,
      at peace and
         steady...

Like a hiker—
     walking over hills,
        up and down mountains even,
     delighted by
        unexpected fields of beautiful flowers,
     inspired by
       panoramic vistas,
           looking forward to what is on
           the other side of the hill,
            and
             peaceful all the way...

Like a musician—
    amazed and
      fascinated by elderly musicians
     who are still enthralled
       with hearing new music.
      True seekers,
        never tiring of the journey of discovery,
         never feeling like
           "they've heard it all."

     victors of faith...
discovering new friends,
         wherever they are,
   seekers,
      who give to others,
      who live with heart,
      with peace...

Victors of faith recognize and embrace a
responsibility to fully live until
the end of their human lives...
to live and interact as though
this earthly life is *not* all there is...

They see this as a continuation
of their spiritual journey—
as a special time
to pray and inspire others,
especially their loved ones
and the young,
with the gift and legacy of faith and hope.

They are not afraid.
They live with faith and hope,
and in this way, they are truly living.

One dear cancer victor
strongly exemplified this attitude toward living...

He was a friend to many,
a teenager who played football and worked in a
local pizzeria,
always enthusiastic about other people.
He stayed in his hometown,
married, and raised a family.

An energetic person,
this man loved people,
never missing an opportunity to give
encouragement to others...

Proud of his son and daughter,
he spoke of his son's
athletic accomplishments and

also mentioned to a doctor friend in passing that
          his daughter, who was then in seventh grade
                    and getting straight A's in school,
                    was interested in medicine...

          "You'll get that scholarship someday," he often told
                              his daughter,
                    referring to a newly instituted scholarship at the
                    local high school for students with aspirations
                    in the field of medicine...
                              it was something he had
                              told her since she was in
                              seventh grade,
                                        and he never stopped
                                        encouraging her.

Several years later,
          still in his 30s,
          he developed symptoms and was diagnosed with cancer.

          This Victor of Faith faced his difficult situation,
                    like so many other victors,
                    with faith and courage,
                    with spirits high,
                              grounded in a down-to-earth
                              sense of reality...
                    and yet giving to the end.

Even when undergoing
          treatments,
     he never failed to enthusiastically ask those caring for him,
                              "How you doin'?"

                    Many months later,
                              now physically thin and weakened,
                              lying in bed,

uncomfortable in one position for long,
slightly bent over,
constantly shifting positions,
he still engaged you with
eyes that radiated his friendliness
and enthusiasm.

The night he
passed away,
his words to a visiting doctor were
filled with life and giving:

"You take a break tonight and
watch the Yanks and Red Sox,
Clemens is pitching!"

The doctor assured him
he'd watch the baseball game.

The doctor then smiled and left saying,
"Pray for me, will you?"

"I will....watch Clemens!"

...To care about others first,
a live to the end, give to the end inspiration
that did not go unnoticed...

And this victor's daughter?
Several years later, she was awarded the very scholarship her father told her she would earn!

Her father's encouraging words made a difference in
her young life... the scholarship opened a new door for
her to do research at a cancer institute.

Today she is in medical school,
                        soon to become a doctor.
Maybe her clinical approach to her patients
        will echo her father...

Maybe she will greet her patients with,
                        "How you doin?"

Work, too, has value—
        even God can be found in work...

        "I can find God in my work," said one founder of a
           religious group for lay men and women,
                                Josemaria Éscriva.

        "All are called to be saints, to holiness...
        In this crazy world, there are many wonderful souls...

        I assure you, my children, that when a Christian
        carries out with love the most insignificant daily action,
     that action overflows with the transcendence of God..."

What Wondrous Love is This?

Another time, while he was visiting Rome,
        someone asked Father Escriva:

"Which chapel in Rome do you like the best?"
He responded by simply looking out at
                the busy city street and saying "that one."

"Work like you don't need the money,
Love like you've never been hurt,
Dance like nobody is watching."
                        Satchel Paige,
                        Hall of Fame baseball pitcher

"Don't look back,
something may be gaining on you…"
                        Satchel Paige,
                        baseball pitcher

                Blur the line between work and play…

Whether in a highly acclaimed task or simple service,

anything you contribute matters…

        You won't always be the leader or main contributor,
                that's unrealistic…
                                in athletics,
                                in a profession,
                                in a trade,
                                in music or art,
                                in public service…

                        …it can be sacred,
                                a form of self-giving…

                        We can sanctify our work,
                        and appreciate the work of others.

On Making Rye Bread

To make good rye bread,
it takes a lot more than the main
ingredients of water, flour, and yeast.

Making bread is a lot like making wine.
You've got to age it.
The most important thing is the aging process.
The first step is that you have to have a darn
good sponge,
kfaus in Polish,
a special yeast preparation made with
rye that needs aging.
Some people make the bread too fast.
Good things take time.

Many people were brought up on this bread,
it's a special kind of rye bread with a
distinct flavor.

You know, they call bread the staff of life.
It's true. In order to exist, you've got to have it.

I worked hard,
but got great satisfaction from
producing quality baked goods."

Jack Stomper, baker

"I think it's good to keep out of the spotlight,
but leave behind something of value."

a father's advice to his son

"Don't be consumed by earthly passions,
Make service to others a passion."

Father Paul Keeling

Sometimes a person may work to the end of their life
because their work has so much meaning to them...
that's OK,

It's OK to follow your heart—
to be fully human and fully alive to the end...
living and giving...

"My dad loved his job," a 26-year old daughter emphasized
in her final spoken tribute to her father, who had been
a manager at a [department] store.
She knew it was an important part of who he was,
in addition to the quiet times they spent together,
listening to music
or taking off work to drive her to graduate school...

... we should all be so lucky—that work was as
important to a balanced life as anything else, and that,
in the end, it may be our work memories that become
our fondest.

For those of us who knew [this woman's father], we
feel certain that he had no regrets in his final hours. We
know his wife, daughter and father were first in
his thoughts.
But we also
think that as his life slipped away,
there is a pretty good chance
his mind was also filled with memories
of his store, his co-workers
and his job...

...For some people, work is a big part
     ·   of what makes life worth living..."
"In Death, an Appreciation of Work,"
Tara Parker-Pope and Kyle Pope,
The Wall Street Journal

"There can be no joy of life
without joy of work."
St. Thomas Aquinas

"I would not consider any spirituality worthwhile
     that wants to walk in sweetness and ease
         and run from the imitation of Christ."
St. John Climacus

"These things I have spoken unto you
    that in me you might have peace.
In the world you are going to have tribulation,
but be of good cheer,
I have overcome the world."
John 16:33

Life for God-responsive souls moves from
     a circumference to a center...
The secret of happiness is being centered in
     Someone greater than ourselves...
Such a soul has a wisdom that surpasses all book learning...

"I've read the last page of the Bible.
It's going to turn out all right."
Billy Graham

"Pray for me" are
     often the last words I'll say to someone...
                 it's as simple as that.

"The best way to enjoy old age
is to see in it a time for making up
for the sins that went before,
    and living in hope for the joys that lie ahead.
                    But this takes faith."
                               Fulton Sheen

"No life is too far spent to be recouped.
No lifelong idleness precludes
    a few minutes of useful work in the vineyards
    of the Lord, even in the last few hours of life,
as was the case with the penitent thief."
                               Fulton Sheen

A sign outside a simple, roadside
country church reads:
"Repent!"

But maybe it should have read:
"Forgive!"

Forgiveness is a choice,
not a feeling...

There can be great power and peace,
even in suffering...

One cancer victor
had a long course of disease.

She lived the last year of her life
without a word of complaint,
not one word, ever.

When she was near death,
    with her husband by her side,
    her now-grown children all gathered to be with her...

She spoke frankly and lovingly,
    and put everyone at ease,
        at peace.
      Even at this difficult time,
        she broke through any anxiety,
        placing her future and theirs in
          God's hands,

She led by example:

      "I have no regrets," she said calmly.
  "I am very thankful.
    I am not afraid.
      Let's enjoy the day."

This victor of faith passed away peacefully.

      "My peace I leave with you,
        my peace I give unto you:
        not as the world giveth,
          do I give unto you.
        Let not your heart be troubled,
        nor let it be afraid."
            John 14:27

Are we living or are we dying?
It's an age old question...
    but from a faith perspective,
      we live up through the last day of our life,
        and then we live a different life...

And throughout life,

we can try offering the biggest and even the smallest
pain, bad mood, trying circumstances,

for the sake of others...

"People are unreasonable, illogical, and self-centered.
    Love them anyway.
If you do good, people will accuse you of selfish
ulterior motives.
    Do good anyway.
If you are successful you win false friends and true
enemies.
    Succeed anyway.
The good you do today will be forgotten tomorrow.
    Do good anyway.
Honesty and frankness make you vulnerable
    Be honest and frank anyway.
People favor underdogs, but follow only top dogs.
    Fight for some underdogs anyway.
What you spend years building may be destroyed
overnight.
    Build anyway.
People really need help, but may attack you if you
help them.
    Help people anyway.
Give the world the best you have and you'll get kicked
in the teeth.
    Give the world the best you've got.
Anyway."

Anyway, anonymous,
hung on wall by Mother Teresa
Sisters of Charity orphanage in Calcutta, India,
as recounted by Dr. Robert Schuller

Enjoy God's gifts and blessings

Give back for all you have been given—
    to the poor, the lonely, the elderly, the sick...

Share gratitude and happiness...
Nobody has it all!

Be glad, rejoice, and thank God...

"Death changes nothing.
If we do not learn to enjoy God now,
      we never will.
If we do not learn to praise and thank and rejoice in
    God now,
      we never will."

Dorothy Day

*"When you get to the top,
send the elevator back down."*

attributed to musicians
Ramsey Lewis and Louis Armstrong
and to basketball player
Charles Barkley

"The measure of life
is not in the heap of goods or honors,
nor days one gathers,

but in the overcoming of hate and despair,
the sharing of kindness,
the celebrations of joy and love that each day offers.

If you want your measure of life to be filled,
pour it out freely."

Beulah Stotter

Sunday
come Sunday...

Eight

The Spirit of an Athlete

Imagine how athletes would feel
                if they knew that there are patients with
                advanced cancer
                who take a break to watch them play...

                This takes some athletes aback.
                They'd never thought of it before.

Modern, multi-purpose sports and entertainment arenas
                advertise their latest, high-tech amenities—
                                skyboxes, catered service, fine dining, club
                                seats, executive seats, extra-wide concourses,
                                unmatched comfort, concession options such
                                as BBQ and gourmet pizza,
                and cutting-edge,
                                technologically sophisticated scoreboards...

        Yet if
        the passion, pathos and live, immediate journey of the
        athletes on the field—or the musicians on stage—
                                isn't evident,
                                and isn't felt by those in the stands,

                        then spectators may walk out,
                                                saying only:

                        "Nice Food."

        But it's possible to have another experience—
                an appreciation
                                of the true spirit of the athlete.

In the same way that
    not all jazz musicians playing an instrument
        play with the genuine spirit of a jazz musician,

    Neither do all athletes on a playing field or court
        play with the genuine spirit of an athlete...

Athletes and teams that play
    with the true spirit of an athlete
        compel you to watch them play,
        to almost be there with them ...

    Not because of any superficial hype,,
    but because you *know* they are giving their all—
                        and it's exhilarating!

The spectator can
    almost feel the energy, the focused intensity,
    the split-second timing and internal rhythm,
        the chemistry and the teamwork...

In these moments.
    you catch the genuine spirit of an athlete...

Whether they win or lose, there's a richness in the struggle...

You—and everyone watching the game with you,
        and everyone watching the game anywhere else—
            witness strength, skill, patience,
                    grace, economy of motion,
            competitive savvy, guile, and aspiration...
                all attributes of great athletes...
                similar to some of the attributes
                        of great jazz improvisation masters,
    and in a greater way,
            similar to some of the attributes of
                the spiritual journeys of victors of faith.

Even silence,
     pauses or hesitations...
          waiting for the right moment...timing...
all are important elements of athletics, music, and truly
                         spiritual journeys...

These quiet elements help foster, for example,
     economy of motion,
          instead of wasted movement,
     focused energy,
          instead of random play or searching,
     paced perseverance,
          instead of early burn-out...

Sadly,
musicians and athletes who lack passion in their performance
     yield spiritless playing,
          polished perhaps,
               but lifeless music,
                   dull games...

     They resemble the following description of a
     so-called happy man,
          but a man who lives without a deeper passion,
          or a sense of meaning and purpose for life:

"Eating like a schoolboy and sleeping like a healthy infant—
a jolly ruddy-cheeked man, without a care in the world,
     unshakably confident to the very end
     that he alone has found the answer to the riddle of life,
that God and man are fools that he has got the better of,
that his way of life is utterly successful,
               satisfactory,
               unassailable.
We must be careful at this point to prefer his conversion."

                                 C.S. Lewis

And isn't this true spirit of an athlete
similar to the true spirit the musician?

"We know a case in which a violinist
        always tried to play as consciously as possible.

From putting his violin in place on his shoulder
        to the most trifling technical detail,
        he wanted to do
                everything consciously,
        to perform in full self-reflection.

This led to a complete artistic breakdown....

Treatment had to give back
        to the patient
                his trust in the unconscious,
        by having him realize
        how much more musical his unconscious was
                        than his conscious."
                        Viktor Frankl,
                        psychologist

This also could be said about
        a golfer struggling with his swing,
        a baseball hitter in a slump,
        or a basketball player
                struggling with his jump shot or foul shot...

Why do we sometimes see a lack of heart in music,
athletics, or life?

Why do some athletes lack heart in the way they compete?

A college basketball coach says that
some athletes play with a fear of losing:

"There's an investment of emotion that's required
in playing at a high performance level.
In order to do that, you have to believe you're going to
win....
But sometimes you don't win, and when you lose, it
hurts.

There are some people who try to avoid the hurt,
to avoid the feeling you go through when you lose,
and that can happen at an early age...

Maybe a kid learns to play and he's pretty good. He's
excited and eager to play his game. But at that game
maybe he doesn't perform well, his team loses...and it
all happens in front of people...
He goes home and cries.
That cry shouldn't relieve you if you're a
competitor.
You've got to have those times when you want to cry...

If you try to avoid the pain of losing, then you'll never win.
You'll be driven by a fear of losing and you won't win...

I first really noticed this when I was a junior college coach.
We had played a game against an opponent that had a
little more talent than we did,
but we had an opportunity to win.

To win would have required a total investment of emotion from our student athletes, and we didn't get that
investment.

The game was very close. We lost. But I noticed that pain
didn't seem to be evident. The loss was dismissed
rather early. There was disappointment, but not a lot of
pain or hurt.

The next day I had a meeting with the team and began to talk
    with them about what it's like to be hurt—not necessarily
    by a sport, but by life...the circumstances in life when
    you really expect an outcome and you don't get it. You've
    invested countless hours of training or preparing for
    it—whether it's a recital, a basketball game, a football
    game, or a relationship—and you don't get the outcome
          you wanted,
                    and it hurts.

Then we talked about what our options are after that.
    Do we now withdraw everything and never invest at all
    in this relationship or this outcome that we desired?
And if we do that,
    we don't experience the pain,
    but we will never experience the joy of winning either,
    the joy of being successful or of having a
              good relationship.

The athletes began to understand that there's some
    similarity involved in life and in how we live it,
    and in how we go after a certain success
          regardless of what it is...

They began to understand that if we don't have a total
    investment of ourselves, if we don't totally believe
    we're going to win,
    we won't be successful...

And if we do have that total investment of our emotions and
    our energies,
    but we fall short of our goal,
        then it's OK to have that pain—
    it's supposed to hurt because that will drive you to
        prepare harder the next time."

Reggie Witherspoon,
basketball coach,
University at Buffalo

"It's not the critic who counts; not the man who points out how the strong man stumbles, or where the doer of deeds could have done better. The credit belongs to the man who actually is in the arena ... who, at best, knows in the end the triumph of great achievement, and who, at the worst, if he fails, at least fails while daring greatly. So that his place will never be with those cold timid souls who know neither victory or defeat."

Theodore Roosevelt

Sports is live action…
    it's human and real,
    it nurtures a connectedness
            without words…
  a shared experience that begins and ends at the same time
          for all spectators, coaches and players.
    It connects people,
        a real-time connection…

Marty Glickman was an Olympic sprinter..
      At 18, in his first year at Syracuse University,
      he was chosen as part of the four-man, 400-yard relay
      team along with Sam Stoller, another young Jewish
                 man, and 5 other sprinters.

That was in 1936,
      and the Olympics were being hosted by Hitler's Germany.

           For two weeks, the U.S. Olympic squad
           prepared diligently in Germany for the relay race.
                They were confident of victory.

           But the day of the qualifying trials,
           Glickman and Stoller were replaced with two other
           runners—Jesse Owens and Ralph Metcalfe.
                Jesse Owens protested that
           Glickman and Stoller deserved to run...
           Glickman pointed out that any combination
                of the seven could win the race
                        by 15 yards.
           Glickman also pointed out to his assistant coach
                that there could be a lot of criticism
                back home if they replaced the
                only two Jewish athletes on the relay team.

The head track coach did not change his decision.
      Glickman and Stoller watched
      the American victory from the stands.

Was that heart-breaking?
      Of course.

      But it didn't keep Glickman down.
           It didn't keep him
                from his dreams.

Marty Glickman went on to
    become an All-American football player.
    And after a brief stint in professional
                football and basketball,
            he became
        the famous broadcast voice
        of the New York football Giants
        and the New York Knicks basketball team.

45 years later,
        Glickman didn't focus on his sad
        Olympic experience when he spoke to young athletes
            at the opening ceremony of New York's
            Empire State Games...

    Instead,
        he told them about the bigger picture
        of what he learned from sports:

                        "Look around you,
        There's nothing better in life
                    than having a goal,
                working hard at it,
                    and *especially* doing it with your friends!"

People long for genuine fellowship, whether in the work place
        or in community...
        even many former pro athletes say that the thing they
        miss most is the fellowship with teammates,
                that human, striving together connection with
                other people.

"Where would you rather be,
than right here...right now?"

Marv Levy,
Hall of Fame football coach

The true spirit of an athlete
        like that of a musician,
        reaches far beyond the athlete or musician himself—

        One night a patient with advanced cancer
was confined to an isolation room due to the nature of his
                                        treatment.
He invited me to watch a college basketball game with him—
        the Syracuse University Orange and the
                                Providence College Friars.

        The two fans watched the game together that night—
        both knowing that it would
                begin and end for athletes and spectators alike
                at the same time,
        both enjoying the human connectedness of sports.

        human,

        real,

        connected...

The morning after the Boston Red Sox lost the
        1986 World Series to the New York Mets,
        several signs were placed around the
        Dana-Farber Cancer Institute.

The signs announced:

EMOTIONAL SUPPORT GROUP MEETING

— FOR RED SOX FANS —

12 Noon, in the Conference Room

Hot dogs & lemonade

sponsored by Psychosocial Support Staff

Was this a cruel joke on Red Sox fans—
    just two days after a ground ball
        had passed through the legs of the Red Sox
        first baseman and gallant warrior Bill Buckner
        during the critical Game Six loss to the Mets?

At noon,
    curious staff, including doctors and nurses,
    and curious patients,
        several in wheel chairs with poles supporting
        their intravenous fluids and medications
        —all lifelong Red Sox fans—
            filled the conference room.

In front of the crowded room stood several members of
the psychosocial support staff—social workers and clergy—
and two former Red Sox players.
The staff opened up the discussion.

Both doctors and patients expressed
    their hurt and frustration,
        their grief,
            that the Red Sox had lost.

One young leukemia doctor
> told of attending Red Sox games since childhood with
> his father.
> He expressed his anger and frustration at what he
> thought was reckless base running by the Red
> Sox throughout that World Series.

It was an odd sight
> to see this young doctor standing next to
>> an older leukemia patient in his wheel chair,
>> with several intravenous lines attached to him.

>> The patient cut the young doctor off...
> Everyone thought,
>> "It's time for perspective,
>> after all, it's only baseball."

But to everyone's surprise,
> this patient joined in with even greater anger and
> frustration, as he blamed the third base coach,
> Don Zimmer, for recklessly sending runners
>> around second and third base
> only to be thrown out throughout the Series.

>> On that day,
>> in that room
there were no patients or doctors or nurses—

>> only Red Sox fans.

The genuine spirit of an athlete—
> motivated by the pursuit of victory,
> not by the fear of losing...

The game—
>a shared experience,
>that begins and ends at the same time
for all players, coaches and spectators,
>>human and real,
>>a nurturing connectedness
>>among people.

>True enjoyment,
>satisfaction,
>or victory
>>is found in the pursuit,
>>>in the people,
>>>in all parts of the journey,
>>>"on earth as it is in heaven."

As one song says:
>"Don't wait until the battle is over to shout..."

>>...cancer victors often look back and
>>>appreciate the journey.

*"Riches, pleasures, honors,
joys and titles are desired
merely because they can
intensify the joy of living.
Of all our treasures, it is life
that we surrender last."*

>>>>Fulton Sheen

"Success is peace of mind,
which is a direct result of
self-satisfaction in knowing
you did your best
to become the best
you are capable of becoming."

John Wooden
Hall of Fame College
basketball coach, UCLA

The next best thing to playing and winning
is playing and losing...

There is life after the final buzzer...

"I have fought a good fight,
I have finished my course,
I have kept the faith."

II Timothy 4:7

Playing with heart,
is playing with
the true spirit of
an athlete...

Nine

Life Beyond the Final Buzzer

The game buzzer rings...
   There's no going back.
     no more changes to be made,
     no more plays to strategize...
      it's done,
        over,
         finished...

           Now what?

But is it *really*
  done,
    over,
      finished?

Victors of faith don't think so—
  Instead, they challenge us, by asking:

      What final buzzer?
      Or, rather, which one?

There are events in life that change us, alter us, affect us,
  but there is always something beyond that moment—
  something else on the other side of the bridge,
       so to speak...

After all, when has your life ever truly stopped?

Not when you leave a place where you've lived,
             worked or gone to school for a long time...
Not when the big performance ended,
Not when the big game was won or lost,
Not when you graduated from high school,
Not when you graduated from college,
Not when you passed the bar or earned a promotion,
Not even when a team won the Super Bowl,
             or when you achieved a longtime goal.

There's always something else...
             always.

When the Dalai Lama
             won the Nobel Peace Prize in 1989,
             he stepped up to the microphone on that grand
             occasion to say a few words...

But reporters quickly hounded him with
             the question, "What's next?"

He didn't hesitate to gently guide them back
             to the present moment,
             to the importance of enjoying the
                   present moment.

We may not know what's next,
             but we can be certain there's always
                   something...

Be grateful in our good moods,
and graceful in our low moods.

When athletes play with true spirit,
When they give completely of themselves,
        there can be a let down feeling after the game,
        an emptiness,
        even if they win the game...

        That can happen after other achievements too—
                after the last game of a player's career,
                after a senior prom, or the end of high school
                                                    or college,
        after a long time employee retires,
        after a company goes out of business,
                                    or after being laid off,
        after conquering the highest peak,
        after taking a long-planned and much-sacrificed-for
                                                    trip.

Medical students,
        after having poured years and countless hours of
sleepless nights into their studies, papers, research,
        internships and learning,
                when they finally achieve their dream of
                becoming a doctor...
                can feel a little disappointed,
                it's not exactly what they expected,
                        it's a let-down.

This isn't all there is.

A goal that consumed them for so long,
                    now achieved,
                    but a bit empty...

There are lots of perceived "final buzzers" in life,
          yet none of them really are final at all...

Even speaking of such things in terms of finality—
          "the end of a career,"
          "the last concert,"
          "the final day"—
                    can evoke depression.

"Final buzzers" are just part of the endless journey,
          part of our unique fusion of experiences,
                    our unique collage,
                    our endless song...

                    and not final at all.

We can put great pressure on ourselves,
                    when it isn't necessary
                              or even reality.

Great happiness,
great sadness—
          it isn't all there is...

Our truest sense of home continues on the other side
of the bridge,
          the ultimate Sunday—
                    the rest is all just part of life.

The Lord of happiness doesn't want anything
          less than happiness for our lives.
But happiness is never complete in this earthly life—

In many ways, the thrill of human passion is in the journey
                                              itself.

Do you *really* believe in the Resurrection?
Victors of faith began living for eternity,
                    today,
                    now,
                              this moment—
                              in whatever task
                              they find themselves,
                              in whatever situation...

            "I shall spend my heaven
            doing good upon earth."
                    St. Therese of the Child Jesus

During one spring training season,
          Yankee manager Yogi Berra passed by
the Yankee club house
          and saw some players watching
          a Steve McQueen movie.

McQueen had just recently died.

Yogi Berra, the sage Coach and Hall of Famer noted,
seriously,

"Hmmm...he must have made that before he died."

"You know, there is definitely life after the final buzzer,"
     says Coach Reggie Witherspoon.
                         "Sometimes that buzzer can go off
                                   and you win.
          But you have to realize that there is
                    life after that win
                    and there is life after a loss.

And I'll tell you what,
the ones who have difficulty dealing with a loss
are the same ones who will have difficulty dealing with a win."

"Do not weep,"
          St. Dominic said to those around him on his deathbed,
                    "I shall be of more use to you in heaven
                              than in my lifetime."

     "Is this heaven?"
          "No, it's Iowa."
                         Shoeless Joe Jackson and Ray Kinsella
                         in the movie Field of Dreams

     "This isn't heaven;
          we didn't expect it to be."
                         cancer victors from a rural county in upstate New York

     "This isn't heaven;
          so don't expect it to be."
                         Max Lucado,
                         When God Whispers Your Name

After the sudden, unexpected death of a mother,
     her son, who was deeply affected by

the crushing event,
    made the simple comment:
        "This is her Good Friday,
        but we know that her Easter Sunday
        is coming in a few days."

For every Good Friday,
    there is an Easter...
There must be Good Fridays
    to have Resurrection—
    the Crucified Christ spirituality is as important
as the Risen Christ spirituality...
        but the song,
        the journey,
        is without end...

"My uncle Alex Vonnegut,
    a Harvard-educated life insurance salesman
    who lived at 5033 North Pennsylvania Street
    taught me something very important.
    He said that when things were really going well,
    we should be sure to *notice* it.

He was talking about simple occasions,
    not great victories:
maybe drinking lemonade on a hot afternoon in the shade,
    or smelling the aroma of a nearby bakery,
    or fishing and not caring if we catch anything or not,
    or hearing somebody all alone playing
    a piano really well in the house next door.

Uncle Alex urged me to say this outloud
       during such epiphanies:
           'If this isn't nice, what is?'

...OUR TOWN, by the late Thornton Wilder...
       I had already watched it with
           undiminished satisfaction
           maybe five or six times.

       And then this spring my
           13-year-old daughter, dear Lily,
           was cast as a talking dead person
           in the graveyard of Grover's Corners
           in a school production
       of that innocent, sentimental masterpiece...

What hit me really hard that night, though,
       was the character Emily's farewell
       in the last scene,
           after the mourners have gone back
           down the hill to their village,
           having buried her.

She says, 'Good-by, good-by, world.
       Good-by, Grover's Corners...
       Mama and Papa.
       Good-by to clocks ticking...
           And Mama's sunflowers.
       And food and coffee.
           And new-ironed dresses
           And hot baths...
       and sleeping and waking up.
         Oh, earth,
           you're too wonderful for
           anybody to realize you.

> Do any human beings ever
> realize life while they live it?—
> every, every minute?'"
>
> *Kurt Vonnegut,*
> *Timequake*

What a Wondrous Love is This...

Eternal life,
Come Sunday—
    no buzzers,
    no end...
        true joy,
        true home.

Ten

Play Right Through It

A time for work,
> A time for play,
>> A time for everything under heaven...
>>> *cf. Ecclesiates 3:1-8*

Cancer victors remind us that life is short...

> They tell us to keep enjoying life,
during the seasons of inconveniences we may face,
during the pursuit of a goal or an accomplishment.

> Make time for fun in our lives,
>> some refreshing moments...

Cancer victors
are not paralyzed by fear or anxiety...
> They don't stop living or enjoying life...

They break big projects
> or a long series of testing or treatment
>> into little steps,

They take a rest now and then,

> They plan something enjoyable as a reward...
>> and often
>>> they play right through it.

Sometimes victors of faith
        just keep doing what
              they've been doing—
                    the work and activities
              that have meaning and satisfaction for them.
                    They don't look back,
              they just move forward
                        and do what's necessary.

As a hearty
        farm wife remarked
        in her matter-of-fact way:

            "What's the big deal?"

            "I had surgery,
            chemotherapy
            and radiation,
                  and I *still* had to help manage the farm."

Not only that,
  she also had to
  take care of her husband,
        who had recently
        suffered a stroke.

            "I had to help take care of my husband,
                    the farm,
                    and everything else…

            What's the big deal?"

            Consider the high profile achievers,
                celebrities,
                public personalities,
                movie and TV stars,

famous athletes and musicians,
government leaders,
and the super-wealthy,
all those who've developed
a reputation for fame or success...

when the cameras and lights are off,
they each live life like everybody else.

They might keep up a public image.
They might not talk about
how they plan breaks into their busy schedules,
But they do it,
in simple ways,
just like everyone else can...

In fact,
after a diagnosis of cancer,
many of these
highly successful people have turned to
simple, humble victors of faith
for inspiration.

One patient,
a highly successful,
well-respected and wealthy individual,
shared his wisdom of achievement
and successes,
while undergoing follow-up care...

Yet what he didn't say
spoke volumes about his success,
for within minutes after his visit,
he was strolling peacefully
along the harbor with his wife,
each with an ice cream cone in hand.

Another time,
      again within minutes of a hospital visit,
          he simply enjoyed
          a deli sandwich with his wife
on a bench
          watching the Swan Boats glide by
          in the lagoon in the Boston Public Garden...

This highly motivated, highly successful man
          planned to take breaks,
          to make time for a little fun after his treatment.

      Common moments,
          simple moments...
          ways that we, too, can play right through it...

"Pray, hope, and don't worry.
Worry is useless.
God is merciful and will hear your prayer."
                        Padre Pio

Another patient,
      a high-powered business executive
      played right through his daily cancer treatments in
                      a different way:

      Immaculately groomed,
          this man showed up promptly at the
      scheduled time for each of his outpatient treatments...

Nearly always he arrived mid-conversation,
                  on a cell phone.

He acted like these treatments were
    little more than a necessary inconvenience in his life...

    When he arrived, he folded his clothes neatly,
        did what was required,
            and then picked up his phone and
            resumed his business conversation.

He was not rude or impatient,
    he did not dwell on fears...

Instead, he lived life like a victor of faith.

The way he dealt with cancer treatments
        is probably how he dealt with other
                annoyances in his life,

        he played right through it.

Other victors
go to the movies,
    catch a game,
    get together with some friends,
    plan a hike or a short trip,
        enjoy nature and the outdoors,
      go to the mall,
      have their favorite ice cream sundae
        or pizza...

*"I don't mind the grey skies,
'cuz they're just grey clouds
passing by..."*
Come Sunday, Duke Ellington

they continue to live and enjoy life...
                they play right through it.

Some people think of
                their outpatient cancer testing or treatment
                in the same way they think of
                        a car tune-up appointment,
                                a shopping errand,
                        or going to the dentist—
                                in a few hours,
                                it will be all over,
                        and they'll be doing something else
                        that's much more meaningful.

One 90-year-old woman
                recalled that she'd been treated 40 years ago
                                for breast cancer—
                "It seemed like a big deal at the time," she said,
                "but when I look back now,
                                it was just a blip on the screen."

        Our modern lives are so fast and busy,
                so filled with things to do and places to be—

Victors of faith take advantage
                of any slow or waiting time
                        to dream new dreams,
                                make new plans,
                                re-invest in family and friends,
                                or maybe to be still.

Some patients practically skip out of the hospital
after a treatment or appointment
because they are looking forward
to a special treat
they'd planned the night before...

Be good to yourself,
Treat yourself now and then,
It's OK.
It's what all the most successful,
most powerful
people in the world do,
whether or not they let you know;
maybe it's part of their technique for success...

But,
playing right through it
is not merely positive thinking...

There's the story of
a basketball team that was losing all its games one season.

The coach searched for ways to motivate his team.

In the locker room before the game
the coach walked up to his point guard and said:
"When you go out there tonight,
I want you to pretend that you're
the best point guard in the world!"

Then he talked to the big man on the team,
"When you go out there tonight," he told him,
"I want you to pretend you're the best center
in the world—
the best ever!"

The team rallied
    and charged out of the locker room.
        The crowd could sense
            their positive attitude and energy.

        ...but they didn't win.

        They lost again,
            this time by 40 points.

        In the locker room after the game,
        no one was more dejected and upset
            than the coach.

The big center lumbered up to him,
    put his arm around the coach's shoulders,
    and said,

    "Coach, why don't you just pretend we won the game?"

Positive thinking alone isn't enough.
It won't carry you through to the other side...
        Perspective and preparation are key.

"The key is to prepare well, and to gain understanding
    and perspective about your opponent or about
    a situation.

    If things don't turn out as you planned, you go back and do
        it again,
        only this time you do it for the new situation:
            re-prepare,
            re-understand,
            and gain new perspective.

I won't tell you that I block out bad circumstances
or somehow rise above them.
I don't. No one does.
No matter how an athlete or coach's face looks to the
public eye,
no one blocks it out.

You go through the fire like everyone else,
on and off the playing field.
As a coach, you do your homework.
You're prepared for your opponent.
You get focused on what you have to do
and don't get fretful over the distractions.

That goes for anything in life.
You have to ride out the challenges, the obstacles,
and the circumstances that come your way.
Worry adds nothing."

Coach Marv Levy,
Hall of Fame football coach

Victors of faith prove to us that
it isn't the cards we've been dealt in life that
bring us down or build us up...

Instead, it's how we play those cards,
what we do with them,
that's what matters...

They realize that
     there's a higher power at work in our lives—
     a loving God…
          and that makes all the difference…

They remind us of the angels in the Bible
who came bearing good news,
     prefacing their remarks with the phrase
          "Be Not Afraid"…

     Victors of faith are not afraid to keep enjoying their
               lives.
     They do not live with a fear of losing.

The journey is not an even road.
There will be ups and downs—
     momentum—
just as in an athletic contest,
     an entire season,
     or even a musical performance.

     Sometimes
         everything seems to be
         going your way,
         almost like spontaneous chemistry—
         you're on a roll,
         and you know it…

     But other times,
         it's a struggle,
         nothing's clicking—
     it can even change mid-game,
         or mid-season,
         or mid-anything in life…

"If I feel like I'm
just playing notes…maybe I don't feel the
rhythm or I'm not in the best shape… I'll
try to build things to the point where this inspiration is
happening again, where things are spontaneous
and not contrived. If it reaches that point again,
I feel it can continue—it's alive again.
     But if it doesn't happen, I'll just quit, bow out."

John Coltrane

Do even highly trained athletes
have to deal with changes in momentum?

"Absolutely," says one college basketball coach.

"I think that momentum is often dictated by crowd
noise. Sometimes it can cause a severe change in momentum that goes against a team. It can cause self-
doubt to creep in. Then fear tends to accelerate a little
bit. Then the crowd noise and sometimes the unfa-
miliarity with the arena you're in causes a momentum
change that can dictate the outcome of a game…
Sometimes, if you have a more experienced and older
team, and often, a team with a real strong Christian belief, you'll get through these severe momentum changes
a little better."

Why will these teams get through the momentum changes
        better?

"Even before the game or season,
I think they have already developed a perspective on
playing through changes in momentum…

You know, there's a song
that says *Don't wait 'til the battle is over to shout.*

They've already claimed the victory.
They've already done enough studying.
They've done enough of the background that keeps
them strong.
They've already gone through things where they believe
in something that isn't right there in front of
them—
it's a spirit...
And it gives them enough of a belief that it isn't
them against the world,
there's Someone who will bear their burdens."

Coach Reggie Witherspoon

Victors of faith
have already claimed the victory...
They take time to enjoy life,
to even play right through
the inconveniences
and necessities of life...

Eleven

Losers in Disguise

Many seasoned and successful people
enjoy sharing the fruit of their years
with younger people,
and they often offer this advice:

Don't get down on yourself,
We're all just losers in disguise.

"I'd never join any club
that would have me for a member."
Groucho Marx

"Now when I bore people at a party,
they think it's their fault."
Henry Kissinger,
on the virtues of being famous

Wear the right clothes,
Have the right image,
Put on the right facial expression—

Looking for prominence or status?
Will it really make a difference?

"Accelerating from 0 to 60 mph
in a few seconds
slams the body backward
with powerful sensations,
but going 60 for hours on the interstate
causes so little feeling of speed that we
fight to stay awake...
Thrills have less to do with speed
Than [with] changes in speed."
Ronald Dahl,
psychiatry professor

"Anthropologist Bateson says the
constant quest for novelty means
people miss out on the world around them:

'It's a mistake to assume things are
only stimulating if they're new.

If you're in a meadow filled with
birds singing and plants and insects,
that's a stimulating place to be
even though it'll be the same tomorrow.'

"The trick is learning to experience
familiar things in new ways, she says."
Roy Rivenburg, Los Angeles Times,
"A busy, noisy, stimulating world
produces an ample supply of boredom"

What about being content...
an underrated state of mind these days,
but it's a peaceful way to live...
and it's real.

Jazz musicians can be real.
They can be winners one day
            and losers the next,
            and then they can look up and say,
            "Let's just play the blues, man."
                    As one jazz bass player put it:
                    "If you get a little crap on your face,
                    wipe it off and move on."

We can't fool ourselves
            for long,
            not really...
We can't live pretending,
            our closest friends know who we really are,
            and we know them as well,
                    it's a good thing.

                    "We live with our friends,
                    not with our accomplishments."
                            George Brett, baseball player
                            Hall of Fame induction speech

No one does anything completely alone,
        we need each other...

        People such as struggling and aspiring jazz artists
            don't get pats on the back all the time,
            they aren't constantly praised for their
                            artistic growth...

A lot of people's lives are like that—
           a doctor might get recognition
                    from patients and families,
         but what about the technologists,
                the nurses, the cafeteria staff,
                and so many others?

It's that way in all facets of life—
                          we need each other.
"Why do you pass judgement
           on your brother or sister?
For we will all stand before the
           the judgement seat of God."

                            Romans 14:10

Victors of faith show
           mercy and compassion to those who have
                       offended them.
         To forgive is to live.

"The weak can never forgive,
Forgiveness is the attribute of the strong."
                          Mahatma Gandhi

*"Part of me suspects that I'm
a loser
and the other part of me thinks I'm
God Almighty."*
                          John Lennon

Families and friends
    rely on each other
    for mutual mercy and forgiveness,
       as do people when they fail,
      because each one of us,
        in some sense,
         is a loser in disguise.

Don't be afraid of failure,
    there are no perfect lives among us.

   The most successful people in the world
   are the ones who failed the most
       and failed big
    at things that really meant a lot to them...

   But they humbly accepted their failure,
      saw it as a learning experience,
        and bounced back for another pursuit...

One brother asked the Master,
    "How often must I fall and rise up?"
      The Master replied:
      "Until your death."
           Ignatius Byranchaninov

Many artists and musicians
    say that feeling a little blue is a nice place to be...
      It gives them a sense
      of security and connectedness to others...
        it's a comfortable place to be,
        it fosters creativity,
          and a sense of peace.

Many movie stars, famous coaches,
　　　even political leaders
　　　　　　take time to crash and relax for a bit,
　　　　　　to let their hair grow ...

　　　　　　　　　Some escape to nature,
　　　　　　　　　Some take a trip,
　　　　　　　　　　　Others just become recluses
　　　　　　　　　　　　　　　for awhile...

It's normal,
　　　it's part of the rhythm of life,
　　　　　　the ebb and flow—
　　　no matter what a person's position
　　　　　　　　　or power
　　　　　　　　　　　or money.

　　　We are *all* novices on the spiritual journey of life.

"Learn from the mistakes of others,
　　　you can't live long enough
　　　　　　to make them all yourself."
　　　　　　　　　　　　Anonymous

One hallmark of a great education,
　　　　　　of great educated men and women
　　　is that they become perpetual students,
　　　　　　　novices,
　　　　　　　　　and seekers.

　　　　　Cancer victors tell us
　　　　　　　it's never too late to begin...

How many people discover
    the true and talented seeker in themselves
after their formal high school
       or college education?

    ...sometimes it's after
      ten years on the job,
        or after raising their children...
Even professors and statesmen
    renew their ability to seek
       and find
         beauty and love
during sabbaticals or career changes, or retirement.

A truly wise man is comfortable
    having more questions than answers...

        he keeps alive his sense of wonder,
   and he senses the freshness
      and excitement of being a novice.

"Sometimes I wish I could walk up to my music
     as if for the first time,
    as if I had never heard it before..."
                   John Coltrane

We are all novices on the spiritual journey of life.

"I have a captain who conquered loneliness,
I have a captain who did not push a celestial button;
I have a captain who stumbled to the throne."
                   Fulton Sheen

Life—
        our own life...
                a real and spiritual journey,
                   an endless song,

And we?
             Novices to the end,
            masters of failure,
               losers in disguise...

Twelve

Why Me?

Why *me?*

Why did this happen to me?
What did I ever do to deserve this?

Probably nothing.

You probably did nothing to deserve this,

and you are not alone ...

Think of so many others,
truly wonderful, good,
and successful people
who have been hurt physically or emotionally.

Think of all those who are less fortunate...

Think of abandoned children...
of starving families stretched beyond their limits.

Throughout all of history,
innocent people have suffered
oppression,
the injustice of slavery,
the ravages of war,
famine,
tornadoes,
hurricanes,
fires,
or earthquakes...

You are not alone,
    you are not alone in your suffering...

Instead of crying out,

      Why me?

   some victors of faith
   offer another perspective...

They turn the question around...

     They think of so many other tragic
         and unfortunate situations,
       of so many other people
         who have endured suffering
         throughout the world
    and throughout history
       and ask,

         Why *not* me?

It's not a pleasant thought,
    but it's real.

    It's sobering,
    born of a mature faith...

    Not "why me?"
    but, "why not me?"

       And victors of faith
         continue to
      count their blessings...

"If you are without shoes,
go find a man without any feet."
Chinese proverb

"Today I consider myself the luckiest man on the face of the earth."
Lou Gehrig, New York Yankee
Hall of Fame baseball player,
in his final speech in Yankee Stadium
as he suffered from a progressive disease

Mercy, Mercy, Mercy

Imagine...
If all the souls of the faithful departed,
and all the living, earthly souls,
were gathered together...

We, the living,
would be not only comparatively few in number,
we would be lost in the crowd.

Although people often try to block
suffering or loss from their lives,
sometimes they can use
that hurtful memory
as a source of inspiration or
as a motivation
to increase their compassion.

How much more
      do we appreciate
         the things we take for granted each day,
            only after we've lost them,
               even if they are lost
                   for just a little while?
But victors of faith
      don't take life for granted...

When loss comes,
      they don't feel singled out,
        or punished,
        or like the world
           is against them...

Instead,
      victors of faith see themselves
      in fellowship with so many others,
        who have suffered and lost,
        who have persevered,
           in communion with Christ
             in His life and passion ...

They are grateful for the things they do have,
      and complain less about what they don't have.

They don't let themselves
      become consumed with
        feeling cheated,
        angry, or upset.
        They are not afraid...

        They live knowing
          that this is not all there is...

They translate their sufferings into
hope,
love,
a spiritual fellowship
with others.

They have faith that
there is a loving God with them…

Something and Someone is far beyond
this present suffering—

true happiness,
true love,
true joy…

"You know…sometimes we're not prepared for adversity.
When it happens, sometimes we're caught short…
We don't know exactly how to handle it when it comes up.
Sometimes we don't know just what to do when adversity takes over…
And I have advice for all of us.
I got it from my pianist Joe Zawinul, who wrote this tune…
and it sounds like what you're supposed to say when you have that kind of problem —
It's called "Mercy, Mercy, Mercy."

Introduction to "Mercy, Mercy, Mercy"
Julian "Cannonball" Adderley
jazz musician and former school teacher

"I don't have the answer to why people suffer
or why bad things happen to good people,
      it's a mystery to me.
But I do know that Jesus said,
        'If you carry your cross and follow me,
      I will make a place for you in heaven.
      My peace I give unto you.'"

sermon

St. Mary's Church, Batavia, N.Y.

Easter Sunday 1998

Why me?...

It's hard to comprehend sometimes,
      how can God allow suffering—

      But victors of faith believe that
      He has a universal plan for happiness
      and it includes all peoples,
           all walks of life...

Not according to our plan,
      but according to his loving plan for all of us.

Why not?

Come Sunday...

Thirteen

Invest in Your Fortune 500

How many people do we pass by
or interact with regularly
during a week?

These are people with whom we
talk casually,
stand in line,
at a store,
at a coffee shop,
at church...

people we see at our work place,
or a restaurant,
or when we shop,
or go to a game...

people who just happen
to be part of our
regular,
ordinary,
everyday experience
of life and work...

If you really think about it,
we probably interact with about 500 people a week—
our Fortune 500...

How often do we take for granted
the hidden treasures of these people,
hidden treasures that surround us every week...

Sometimes people
        can become self-absorbed,
                preoccupied
                        with status or achievement,
        or with personal hurt
                or injured pride,
                        to ever acknowledge
                        those who surround them every week.

                But victors of faith
                        do notice,
        they invest
                in their Fortune 500...

Imagine the difference
                it makes
        when we invest in
                those who are around us each week—
                                our own Fortune 500...

                if we invest a smile,
                        a kind word,
                        a thank you,
                                a listening ear,
                                an understanding nod...

        "Be kind,
                for everyone you meet is fighting a great battle."
                                Philo of Alexandria
                                Jewish philosopher

"People with clenched fists cannot shake hands."
                                Indira Gandhi

It's true,
                no matter what your position in life,
                the people who are around you every week
                have a place in your life too—

your Fortune 500 may not be
your close friends,
or family,

but they are there
for a reason...

and after the last day of school,
at a job,
or in one town before you move away,
you may realize
that they were a part of your life—

did you get to know their names?

"No man is an island,
No man lives alone,
Each man's joy is joy to me
Each man's grief is my own
We need one another,
So I will defend
Each man as my brother
Each man as my friend."

John Donne

Many nurses and aides
are caring,
single or married mothers,
very busy people—
who could consume their lives
with their spouses, children,
boyfriends, parents, or friends,

and many have their own
sick loved one to care for,

their own personal financial
              and health issues,
and their own personal searches for happiness...

Yet how powerful is the nurse
        who consoles the family of
              a child with leukemia
              by showing
                    heartfelt empathy as
                    she describes her personal experience
                          with her own child who
                          underwent cancer treatment....

The nurses and technologists
are often like angels
        in what they do routinely...
                    quiet victors of faith.

Even a young nurse's aide
        exemplified this so well...

            A patient had just passed away peacefully.

As the family stepped outside the room
        and were consoled by the nurse,
              this young nurse's aide came into the room
                                all alone.

    She quickly and quietly did what was needed.

She cleaned the body,
        tidied up the room,
              and placed the loved one
              in a position of quite repose,

              She thoughtfully added
                          little touches—

a new clean bedspread,
　　　arranged flowers on
　　　　　the adjacent bed stand,
　　　and delicately
　　　　　placed a few flowers in the hands
　　　　　　　of the deceased woman.

She then gently ushered the family in,
　　　　　and left,
　　　　　　just as quietly
　　　　　　　and as unassuming
　　　　　　　as she had entered.

It was beautiful...
　　　so caring,
　　　so giving.
　　　The family didn't even catch the young
　　　　　　nurse's aide's name,

　　　yet they will never forget her...

　　　an angel,
　　　　　a beautiful rainbow
　　　　　amidst passing grey clouds.

This nurse's aide was also
　　　among the Fortune 500 of every doctor
　　　　　　　and nurse
　　　　　　and administrator
　　　　　who was
　　　　　　blessed to work around her.

How many times a day
do things like this happen?
　　　　　More often than we realize!

An ordinary man,
    a teaching doctor,
        made a strong impact
            on his young protegés...

        As he took his students
            on hospital rounds,
            he was always sure
            to include
    a very careful and caring
            visit to someone
            who was dying...

Afterward,
    this excellent doctor and teacher
    would gather his students
        and tell them
        how important it was
to check up on each and every one of their patients,
to care for those who were dying
        with the same caring and concern
        as given to those who were healing...

His words
    and his actions

    made a lasting impression.

        Perhaps the heart of education,
        is the education of the heart...

Then there was the simple but dignified old man,
always dressed nicely
    with a coat and tie
    when he walked through town.

This man simply
>greeted each friend and acquaintance,
>old and new,
>>with a wave,
>>>a smile,
>>>and a "Hi George."

At first, some people thought he was crazy.

>But when they spoke to him further,
>he explained,
>>"You're now a member of the George Club."

He took pride that wherever he traveled,
>>even in other states,
>>someone would often recognize him
>>and initiate
>>>a wave,
>>>a smile,
>>>>and a "Hi George."

It was one man's unique way to invest in his Fortune 500.

Investing in your Fortune 500
>is human connectedness...
>>like sports,
>like live music performed by musicians with spirit;
>>it's connecting with others—
>>>it's human and real...

>People long for genuine fellowship,
>>whether in the community or in the work place...

So many former athletes say that the thing they miss most
>>is the fellowship with teammates.
>>Some day
>>we might look back and miss connecting
>>>with those who are around us weekly,

in little ways—
the simple connectedness of life...

"There's nothing stronger than gentleness."
Abraham Lincoln

You may be the light
of someone else's life,
kindred spirits,
for a short moment,
without even knowing it...

a quiet, solid presence,
a short conversation,
two minutes of reassurance...
it doesn't take much
to invest in those
you see every week...
to appreciate your Fortune 500,
and to show it
in little ways.

"Everyone is a reflection
of how he or she is seen by others.
The very way you look at people
can help transform them."
Jean Vanier
Founder of L'Arche,
communities of life with people
who have developmental disabilities

Sometimes in medical centers,
one may pass patients who are near the end of their lives,
among those on wheelchairs or stretchers in a hall
waiting for an X-ray exam or some form of therapy.

To some,
this may appear cold or clinical,

but consider...

it may be like someone's
last trip to the mall,
their last walk around the neighborhood,
or their last visit to the coffee shop or diner.

Seeing the people and activity
around them,
instead of being isolated,
can give them a sense
of feeling connected with others,
of living...

And blessed are those
who invest a little
smile or attention
to this person,
for you may be one of the last people they see.

"Do not neglect to show
hospitality to strangers...
for by doing that,
some have entertained angels
without knowing it."
Hebrews 13:2

"Love done
is what gives value to all things."
St. Theresa of Avila

"In the depth of common worship
it is as if we found our separate lives
were all one life,
within whom we live and move and have our being."
Thomas Raymond Kelly
Quaker teacher

Live Sunday,
        invest in your Fortune 500...

Fourteen

I Am With You

At his death, all the leaders of the world gathered
   to honor his life,
   even those whose countries were at war.
   Every TV network broadcast the funeral.
   Millions crowded into the streets or watched from TV
                        around the world...

   But he did not start off as a world figure.
   He never intended it.
   He never sought power or riches or fame...

   Instead, he started out as boy named Karol.
         He took life one step at a time
            And he walked with confidence—
               with a confidence born of faith...

               He knew joy
               He knew loss

                     ...He lost his mother at a young
   age, a close Jewish childhood friend at the hands of the
   Nazis, and the rest of his immediate family before he
   was 24 years old...

         ... Karol became a young actor, playwright, student
   and avid hiker...known to friends and locals, but not to
   the world...
He studied and became a priest in secret,
during a dangerous and dark time,
         when his beloved Poland suffered greatly under the
      heavy yoke of first Nazi and then communist domination,

...Then suddenly Karol became Pope John Paul II. He was
    thrown into the international spotlight... serving the
    world for 25 years, during which he survived
    an assassin's bullet and later personally forgave
    his assassin in prison.

                  John Paul II tirelessly traveled ...
                  reached out to the youth and to people
                  of nearly every race and country in the
                  world...

                  In the words of security guards and
                  those assigned to travel with him in
                  various countries, this elder man
                  drew more raw enthusiasm than
                  popular rock stars...

and in the end,
    he bore the cross of Parkinson's disease in his old age
                          with great dignity...

And all his life
    he repeatedly echoed
        "Be not afraid!"

John Paul II, in radiating joy, warmth and peace
    —even amid great personal sufferings and vocational
    demands—testified to
        an Abiding Love for each one of us,
        a Love not of this world...
        a Love that we could have confidence was
                  always with us—

                Why?

Because he believed what the victors of faith believe.

"...I am with you always,
even unto the end of the world."
Matthew 28:20

"He meant what he said..."
Fulton Sheen,
regarding Christ's words in Scripture

Comfort and consolation
aren't only for the patient,

but for caregivers too—
the healthcare professionals,
the family, and
extended family and friends...

Imagine—
If everyone just gave their 1%,
it would add up to 100% in no time...

It's true in every aspect of life,
in team sports,
in work,
in family life,
in charitable projects,
in caring for someone in need...

Victors of faith help each other carry
their crosses...
and every little bit helps.

Five minutes of teamwork
can be larger than any one of us
working alone.

Just being there
can make a difference...

      not worrying about what to say,
        or what to do,

but,
   instead,

    just simply
      being there,
giving our 1%...

The anticipation alone
    may provide comfort and fellowship,
and it may also provide
    a small bridge over troubled waters...

      In some ways,
   the lift and momentum
     that a person
     may feel from knowing that
     family and friends are
       praying or rooting for them

   is similar to
a sense of lift and momentum
     that athletes experience
       from a crowd of cheering fans
      during a game.

Prince of Peace

But it's not like a 30-minute TV show—
  things take time...
    falling in love,
    solving problems,
    becoming friends,
      even diagnosing an illness,
       or caring for one who needs help...
         it's just reality.

  Many cancer patients go through
    weeks of testing before diagnosis,
    the treatment may span months...
    step by step,
      it's a process,
      but it's just part of life—

and you can't hold your breath through it all,
      you must keep living!

    ...life is for the living

Cancer victors teach us to take life as it comes,
    one day at a time
    one step at a time...

    Even Christ himself
      didn't reveal everything
      to his believers in one sitting...

   He spent time with people,
   he talked with them.
     as they walked from town to town,
     as they patiently waited to haul the
      fishing nets into their boats...

He didn't even launch his ministry
        until he was 30 years old...
        and after his baptism by
          John the Baptist,
       even then,
       he first went to the desert for
         40 days and 40 nights,
         before he began teaching...

Jesus is as close to us today
       as he was to Thomas and his disciples
           on their travels,
          in their daily life,
             in the upper room
             for the Last Supper...

Good things take time,
       victors of faith don't see their lives as
          a race against the clock,

instead,
      they gracefully
        bless each day,
          they take a break when they need to,
          they get refreshed when they need to,
          they play,
           have fun,
            pray...

        They keep their eyes on a
        higher purpose than this world alone—

They know God is helping to carry their burdens
        and their hearts' desires,
        and they thank Him for that...

One song
        sung by the great jazz musician,
        Les McCann, beautifully describes
          this comforting presence:

"This material world
This vale of earthly sorrow
Seems so hopeless
          from day to day
          with no tomorrow

And the one thing we seek is love
               but love eludes you
And you'll find when you trust your mind
                your mind eludes you

        So you're lost
           in the dark
        And you're filled with despair

        And you call
           on your friends
        And there's no one there

        So alone in that silent world
        Deep down inside you

                You discover the Prince of Peace
                  Which to guide you
                Lying deep, deep in your heart
                    sits a King on His throne
                And He's your one faithful friend
                    always there,
                    and yours alone

              And the longer you wait to seek Him out,
                the less you will know what life's about.

And the sooner you take His hand
     the sooner life,
         Life is truly beautiful
              it's beautiful
              so beautiful..."
                  "Prince of Peace"
                  Les McCann,
                  jazz musician

Before the printing press
     was invented in 1450,
         all cultures were primarily oral societies,
             that is,
speaking was the main means of communicating ideas.

         People who taught the faith to others,
                    for example,
             would instruct the listener to "echo" it,
          to repeat it until it was learned by heart,
                to speak and echo,
                  Christ is the Word of God...

         who are we?
         who are we,
              but little echoes of Christ
              Christ, who promised to be
              with us to the end of time...
          that's what victors of faith teach us...

"...the church exists for nothing else
but to draw men into Christ,
        to make them little Christs.
If they are not doing that,
        all the cathedrals, clergy, missions, sermons,
        even the Bible itself,
              are simply a waste of time.

"God became man for
  no other purpose.
  It is even doubtful,
    you know,
    whether the whole universe was created
      for any other purpose."
        C.S. Lewis,
        Mere Christianity

"...In the end, every man is seen as a human being.
  Brilliant musician that he was,
    Eric [Dolphy] was still greater as a person.
    He was thoughtful, gracious,
      and genuinely interested in others...
He knew how to enjoy what came his way, and how to give in
return."   *George Avakian,*
    a eulogy in the magazine, "Jazz"

"There's nothing stronger than gentleness."
    Abraham Lincoln

*"Lying deep, deep in your heart,
  sits a King on a throne
And He's your one faithful friend,
  always there,
  and yours alone."*
    "Prince of Peace"
    Les McCann

It's interesting,
     perhaps surprising to some,
          but many patients say that they felt
          more love, enthusiasm, life, and a sense of spirit,
               in a cancer center,
               than elsewhere…

          they say they'll almost miss
               the spirit of the people—

     But this love and spirit and enthusiasm for life
can be found in other places too…

          it's in the musicians,
             the athletes,
             our families and extended families,

             the men, women,
               and children
     who love life and live it with enthusiasm and faith.

While doctors and nurses care for a patient over a course of
hours or days, others embrace them for a life time—

          the musicians and athletes,
     and all lovers of life
             may underestimate
          their longer term contributions to patients' lives…

   we need each other,
   just as we are…

          In a cancer institute,
             I often tell new staff
               not to become part of the wall,
                  but to bring the outside
                    world in…

Victors of faith teach us to
keep a balance to our lives,
so that we stay fresh and creative...

We help others
when we do our 1%,
or even our 5%...
when we help them carry their burdens a little...
when we show others
that we care,

Not merely with our words,
but with our actions,
even if we can only
give a small percent—

"If you go by feelings and emotions,
you are a yo-yo at the end of the devil's string.

You will be up one day
and down the next.

Live by the intellect and will.
The key to sanctity is determination.

Love is in the will, it is a decision."
Fr. John Corapi

"It's always a feast where love is,
and where love is, God is."
Dorothy Day

Caring and communicating with people
is as important as saving lives...

Just being there,
   even offering your 1%,
   offering your prayers,

      can make a difference
      in another person's life.

Listen,
Follow-up,

and others will
      remember your caring,
   and it will help make
      their burden

      just a little lighter...

and their lives
      just a little bit brighter...

Fifteen

Real Time Spirituality

After Coach Phil Jackson
        won his ninth NBA championship
                as a head coach—
            six with the Chicago Bulls and
            three with the Los Angeles Lakers,
    he paid tribute to
        his first NBA coach,
                the late Red Holzman,
                of the New York Knicks:

        "I said at the start of this year
    that I was dedicating this championship
            to Red Holzman, my mentor.

            I know he'd be thinking
    and praying for me wherever he's at
            and whatever form he's at.
        This is a big moment for me and
                for him."
                                Associated Press

    With the lights, cameras,
            and microphones focused on him,
        in the immediate
                rush and glow
                of the championship victory,

    Jackson's off-the-cuff comments reveal
            a sense of real-time,
            matter-of-fact spirituality...

a spirituality that plays into everyday situations,
and at all moments...

"...and
whatever form?"

Just think...

Tiger Woods
enters his backswing with graceful ease,
recoiling with perfect body control,
and drives the ball straight and long—
his follow-through,
masterful and picturesque...

Michael Jordan
leads the fast break,
dribbles the basketball down the left lane,
veers across the foul line.
With body square to the basket,
he begins his jump shot...
perfect release...
perfect follow-through
and score.

Derek Jeter
fields a hard groundball deep to his right,
on the left field grass,
then,
in one seamless motion,
he jumps up,
rotates his body toward first base and,
like a quarterback jump pass,
he throws the runner out at first base
by a step.

Jackson's comment
about his former coach
sheds new light
when old scouts
and sage coaches
look on at this
athletic prowess
and exclaim:

"Nice Form!"

Coach Jackson's spiritual journey
is worthy of respect...

and equally important,
are the spiritual journeys of

Tiger Woods,
Michael Jordan, Derek Jeter—
and every person—
each on a unique
spiritual journey,
and worthy of respect.

But no matter where you are,
or how you are feeling at the moment,

is life
or
genuine spirituality
ever
truly
static?

"Life is what's happening
while we're busy making other plans."
John Lennon

Have you ever seen
    eye-catching advertising
        headlines such as:

"Are you happy with your career?"

"Are you happy with your finances?"

"Are you happy with your body?"

"Are you happy with your sex life?"

Is anyone *fully* satisfied with anything?

        ...unsatiable desires,
    an endless cycle...

Why not choose to be happy
    with limited desires?

"Happiness is a serious problem."
Dennis Prager

"This isn't heaven,
so don't expect it to be."
Max Lucado,
"When God Whispers Your Name"

"We cannot do great things on earth,
We can only do
small things with great love."
Mother Theresa
of Calcutta

Society will be saved by
those who are not absorbed
by the news of the hour,
but by those
who have eternity in their hearts
and time on their hands...

"I like your Christ.
I do not like your Christians.
Your Christians are so unlike your Christ."
Mahatma Gandhi

"Let us know the tree by the blossoms
and the blossoms by the fruit.
When this shall be made clear to our minds,
we may be more willing to listen to you.
But until then,
we must be allowed to follow the religion
of our ancestors."
Chief RedJacket, 1805
Western New York Seneca Indian

"There are no dogmas in temporal affairs.
To try to set up absolute truths
in matters where the individual has to try
to see things from his own point of view,
in terms of his own interest,
his cultural preference,
and his own experience:
this insults the dignity of man.

Any attempt to lay down dogmas in
the temporal sphere leads,
inevitably,
to coercing the consciences of others,
to a failure to respect one's neighbor...

I assure you, my children,
that when a Christian carries out with love
the most insignificant daily action,
that action overflows with
the transcendence of God.

That is why I have told you repeatedly
and hammered away time and time again
at the idea that the Christian vocation
consists in making heroic verse out of
the prose of each day.

Heaven and earth seem to merge,
my children,
on the horizon.
But where they really meet is in your hearts,
when you sanctify your everyday lives."

Josemarie Escriva
"Christ is Passing By"

Our everyday actions and thoughts can be forms of prayer...
to help us live life
with perspective,
with
real time
spirituality.

One day a young doctor
walked by a small exam room in radiology,
on his way to lunch,

on a very routine day,
talking with friends along the way.

He was called into the room by
a radiology technologist,
to help a young patient he had never met before...
They were all the same age—
the doctor, the patient and the technologist...

The mass on the patient's chest radiography was huge—
a tumor had wrapped
around her heart and trachea,
but there was no time
for further interpretation and diagnosis.

The young woman
began coughing up blood
and the young doctor
did all that could be done—
then he supported her weakened body,
and held her hand...
She held on tightly,
and looked the doctor in the eyes.
"God bless you" was shared.
She smiled,
and passed away.

It all happened so fast.

...her parents were grateful
when the doctor later shared
the story of their daughter's
peaceful passing—
but something far beyond
the three young people had happened...

a blessed moment,
a moment rich with
unrehearsed,

           real time
           spirituality.

When asked about the Christian faith,
        Paul responded,

          " 'We look not at what can be seen
but at what cannot be seen,
for what can be seen is temporary,
     but what cannot be seen is eternal.' {*2 Corinthians 4:18*}
     The things we cannot see are paramount,
       and do not change
       -those about which Jesus taught.
          Can we see truth, justice,
          forgiveness, or love? "
                 Jimmy Carter

"Patience...
is not just waiting until something happens over which
       we have no control:
          the arrival of the bus,
          the end of the rain,
          the return of a friend,
          the resolution of a conflict.

Patience is not a waiting passivity
       until someone else does something.

Patience asks us to live the moment to the fullest,
to be completely present to the moment,
       to taste the here and now,
       to be where we are,

When we are impatient
　　　　　we try to get away from where we are...
　　　　as if the real thing will happen tomorrow,
　　　　　　　later,
　　　　　　　and somewhere else.

　　　Let's be patient and trust
　　　　　　that the treasure we look for
　　　　　　is hidden in the ground on which we stand."
　　　　　　　　　　　Henri Nouwen

Real time spirituality...
　　　　matter-of-fact spirituality
　　　　living life *with heart,*
　　　　　　　and with faith in
　　　　　　　　　Sunday...

Sixteen

Simplicity

I cannot bring myself to hunt through books
for beautiful prayers.
There are so many of them
I get a headache...

I cannot possibly say them all
and do not know which to choose,
I behave like [a child] who cannot read:
I tell God very simply
what I want
and He always understands.

For me,
prayer is an upward leap of the heart,
an untroubled glance towards heaven,
a cry of gratitude and love
which I utter from the depths of sorrow
as well as from the heights of joy."

St. Therese of Lisieux,
a young Carmelite nun who died at age 24,
known for her 'little way' of spiritual childhood.

"Our Lord needs from us neither great deeds nor profound
thoughts. Neither intelligence nor talents.
He cherishes simplicity."

St. Therese of Lisieux

"Jesus brought a message that
spoke to the deepest longings of the human heart...
simply,
'Love God, love People.'" *John Ortberg*
pastor and author

Young children know
    only two times:

       the Now

          and

       the Not Now...

            For children, living in
            the present moment is simple,

but
the older we are,
the harder it can be
to keep our thoughts
in the present.

"*Many wealthy people are little
more than
janitors of their possessions.*"

Frank Lloyd Wright, architect

"Live in the now.
It is a gift from God...

Living in the past or future
causes anxiety and depression."
Fr. John Corapi

Some victors of faith
    find that
        keeping focused
            on the present
                is how they best enjoy life,
        how they let grey clouds pass,
            how they can embrace
                those around them.

One cancer victor
         exemplified this so well,

This beautiful and
         loving lady had clearly lived
         a life filled with close family
                        and friends.

                   She was the queen of her family,
not only to her husband, her daughters and sons,
    but also to her grandchildren, in-laws,
                   and her extended family.

When it became clear
    that her earthly journey
        was nearing an end,
  she gathered
      her family together cheerfully
    and she guided them,
        individually and
            in small groups,
      frankly and
        simply:

      "I have faith.
    Let's enjoy this day together,
        like a holiday.
    Let's not worry about the past or the future."

      "Let's not struggle with words,
  just a simple 'I love you'
      and a simple 'God bless you'
        are all we need."

      There were no questions.
Everyone
was put at ease by
      her simplicity,
      her inner beauty of spirit,
      her legacy
        of genuine inspiration...

The simplest of prayers...

Now I lay me down to sleep,

I pray the Lord my soul to keep.

If I should die before I wake,

I pray the Lord my soul to take.

Amen.

Soothing in its simplicity,
           the simplicity of a child...

"Pray for me,"
 are often the last words
 I'll say to someone...
   it's that simple...

   In the words of one Harvard doctor,
   observing work in a cancer institute:
   "You're with some future saints,
    what a privilege!"

Cancer victors,
victors of faith
tell us not to be hard on ourselves,

to be thankful for all we have,
to cherish those around us,

to appreciate the beauty of nature around us,
to fill our thoughts and lives with

gratitude,

love,
and
peace...

simplicity...

Seventeen

No Greater Love

""Love conquers all things

> let us too
> give in to love."
> > *Virgil*
> > *"Ecologues"*

> When we are in love,
> nothing else
> seems to matter...

> Love is
> the greatest power of all...

> but in your life to come
> you will experience
> the greatest love of all...
> > imagine that ...

> "Who then
> shall separate us from
> the love of Christ?

> > shall tribulation?
> > or distress?
> > or famine?
> > or nakedness?
> > or danger?
> > or persecution?
> > or the sword?

...in all these things
we overcome,
because of him that
hath loved us."
Romans 8:35, 37

"No work is hard,
where there is love."
Fulton Sheen

"Love is the inspiration
of all sacrifice,

and love is not
the desire
to have, to own,
to possess—
that is selfishness.

Love is the desire,
to be had,
to be owned,
to be possessed."
Fulton Sheen

Love is about the
other person...

A vivacious young woman
who later
was diagnosed with
chronic neurologic disease,
eventually had to rely
on her husband
for everything

After 20 years
the last few days of which
were in a nursing home,
she became comatose,
and received
a final blessing...

but then

she woke up.

Her husband
noticed that
she grabbed
his hand...

"You don't have to cry,"
this woman
said to her husband.

"Everything is going to be fine."

She spoke in a tone of voice
and with a look
of awareness and
confidence
he hadn't seen in her
for many years.

She peacefully passed away
a few hours later.

"Greater love
hath no man
than this,
that a man
lay down his life
for his friends."
John 15:13

God never asks
for more than you can do—
is it a burden,
a blessing,
or an honor?
...unconditional love
understands beyond
its years,
beyond the surface
or mere appearances...

unconditional love.

"How do I love thee?
Let me count the ways"
Elizabeth Browning

Sometimes
living without someone we love
becomes our way
to give our life,
to show our love ...

"Our highest happiness
consists in the feeling
that another's good
is purchased
by our sacrifice."
Fulton Sheen

"The fulfillment of
Christ's passion
took place the night before He died,
when He,
who was Lord of all things,
had nothing to leave
in His last will and testament
except that which
no one else could give—
Himself."

Fulton Sheen

Reknown Jewish psychologist Viktor Frankl tells this story:
A doctor whose wife had died,
mourned her terribly.
He sought advice from Dr. Frankl.

Dr. Frankl asked him:
"If you had died first,
what would it have been like for her?"

The doctor responded that it would
have been incredibly difficult for her.

Dr. Frankl pointed out that
by having his wife die first,
she had been spared that suffering,
but that now he (her husband) had
to pay the price
by surviving
and mourning her.

Grief can be seen
as the price we pay for love.

For the doctor,
       this thought gave
       his wife's death and his own pain
                       meaning,
          which in turn
              allowed him to deal with it.

His suffering became something more:
       with meaning,
              suffering can be endured with dignity.

Viktor Frankl, psychologist
Holocaust survivor

      Grief—
        the price we pay for love…

There is no greater love
          than giving one's life for another,

          or giving your life more meaning
             because of your love for another.

In little ways,
       cancer victors
    share with
    family and friends,

       and with others
       who care for them,

           a sense of love
        so wondrous,
          and beyond our imagination…

One young man
    was a former
    high school athlete
        and a great sports fan
        of, as they say in Massachusetts,
        all Boston teams.

He worked in
    his family's
    building trade business,
        and loved it.

This young man developed
    advanced cancer
    and was eventually home
        in a coma for four weeks...

But he woke up for an hour one day.
It was completely unexpected.

Family and friends
    were gathered quickly
    from a nearby workplace,

In that brief hour
their son
        and brother
    and friend
        told them three things:

*"I want each of you to know
that we have nothing to fear.
    Everything is going to be all right."*

*"I want each of you to know
that we are all loved."*

"I love each of you
and I always will."

Then he went back
to sleep,
        and passed
away peacefully.

That day,
many lives,
including the lives
    of doctors and nurses,
    who learned later
        of his message,

        were touched by
        his final words...

"...neither death, nor life,
        nor angels,
            nor principalities,
            nor powers,

    nor things present,
            nor things to come,

        nor might,
        nor height,
                nor depth,

            nor any other creature,
shall be able to separate us
    from the love of God,
        which is Christ Jesus
            our Lord."
                            Romans 8:38-39

No greater love,
     Come
     Sunday…

Eighteen

Be Still

Life is precious...

and your unique journey is filled
with precious moments...

but will you notice?

will you enjoy
the journey?

or will you
rush by?

Life,
lived with heart,
is discovery,
improvisation,
an endless song...

and each unique journey
has its own rhythm,
its own pace...

but how will
it be discovered,
without
making time
to listen...

to be still?

"Empty yourself completely
    and sit waiting,
       content with the grace of God,

          like the chick who tastes nothing
          and eats nothing
            but what his mother brings him."
St. Romuald,
Camaldolese monk

          Two days before
           his untimely death,
             rock guitarist Jimi Hendrix pleaded:

          "If you know
            real peace,
              I want to visit
              with you back stage."
Search for Peace,
Robert McGee and Donald Sapough

"Settle yourself in solitude
    and you will
  come upon God in yourself."
St. Teresa of Avila

        "Thou dost keep him in perfect peace,
        whose mind is stayed with Thee."
Isaiah 26

     "I try to teach
       my heart
   to want
   nothing it can't have."
Alice Walker

"The first job
    comes the very moment
    you wake up each morning.

        All your wishes and
                hopes for the day
        rush at you
            like wild animals.

        And the first job
        each morning
                consists simply
                    in shoving them all back;
                    in listening to that other voice,

            taking that other point of view,

            letting that other
                larger, stronger,
                        quieter life
                        come flowing in.

    And so on,
        all day.

            Standing back
                from all your
                natural fussings and frettings,

                    coming in
                    out of the wind."
                            C. S. Lewis,
                            Mere Christianity

"If I had to live my life again,
        I would make a rule to read some poetry
                and listen to some music
                        at least once a week;
        For perhaps
                the parts of my brain
                now atrophied
                would thus have been
                        kept active through use."
                                        Charles Darwin
                                        from Autobiography, 1887

"God is the controller
                God controls.
        Have faith in his mercy,
                Be at peace.
                Be holy."
                                        Father Paul Keeling

"It is good for a man to sit in silence,
and wait for the saving help from the Lord."
                                        Book of Lamentations

"A man's heart is right,
        when he wills
                what God wills."
                                        St. Thomas Aquinas

Fear God,
        in a healthy way—
                not in anxiety,
                but in love,
                        *and you will have
nothing else to fear...*

One husband and wife
    were exceptionally calm
    during the wife's diagnostic tests...

    The husband
        was clearly a
        focused and savvy businessman,
            an achiever and a can-do person...
    but he was remarkably calm.

    His explanation was
        candid and simple:

        "We've had so much tragedy
           in our lives the last five years,
              that we've learned not to worry about stuff
                until it happens
                  or unless we really have to do
                    something about it."

        "I have learned,
           in whatsoever state I am,
      therewith
        to be content."
           Philippians 4:11

"God is unchanging in His love.
    He loves you.
    He has a plan for your life.
        Don't let the newspaper headlines frighten you.
        God is still sovereign.
           He's still on the throne."
           Billy Graham

Many cancer victors
        are high-flying winners,
                very accomplished
                and successful,

The reaction of
        one such patient,
    is typical of many,

                yet he
                stood out in the
                quickness of his discovery...

In reaction to
his diagnosis of cancer,
        this highly motivated patient
                sighed
                and reflected:

                "I had such wonderful plans...

                "I had my six month plan,
                I had my one-year plan...

                        ...my five-year plan,
                        my ten-year plan,...

                                he left the office.

The next day,
    he stopped by,
            energized.

        He,
        like many others
            who live with a high level of energy,
        enthusiastically announced:

"I'm OK now...

"I have a new six-month plan,
I have a new one-year plan,

a new five-year plan,
a new ten-year plan..."

There was nothing to add.
Such patients
        are smarter
        and more energetic
than their doctor.

But there's a sense,
        a dream;

Happiness,
        a more loving longing...

What else do we *truly* need?

Then,
on the third day,
    this same patient returned,
        smiling confidently,
            self-realized,

        a victor,
        a champion...

        "I forgot one plan,
    didn't I?"
            he added,
                "God's plan."

As he left the office
    and walked down the hospital corridor,
  he passed a series of paintings
            created by local artists.

        He stopped
      and paused
          at a painting of grey clouds and a
          storm, with the sun's rays
    breaking through the top of the painting.

Then he continued down the hall,
    now with a smile
    and a new rhythm to his step...
I later walked down the hall
to read the quote at the bottom of that painting...
          "Be still and know that I am God."

"Be still,
    and know
    that I am God."
        Psalm 46:10

      "Have patience with all the world,
        but first,
          have patience with yourself."
          St. Francis de Sales

      Jesus, calm my inner dialog...
      Jesus, I trust in you.

    "In front of Rockefeller Center,
      is found a huge bronze statue
      of Atlas struggling to hold the universe
           on his shoulders.

In the center of St. Patrick's Cathedral,
high over the chapel altar
　　　there is a globe in the left hand
　　　of the Virgin Mary,
　　who has on her lap the child Jesus,
　　upon whom her gaze is fixed in peace and love.
The globe seems to be
　　　　　preoccupying her not at all.
　　　　　She carries it securely but without strain.

Both depict how one might deal with the universe,
　　　　　　　　the world, or life.

One is an unremitting struggle.
In the other it is somehow lost in a
　　　second effort which is far more important,
　　　that of looking upon one's God and loving him."
　　　　　　　　　　Cardinal Edward Egan

You can't enter into the
　　　dialogue of nature,
　　　　　of love,
　　　　　of life
　　　around you,

　　　　　　without listening,
　　　　　　　　attentively,
　　　　　quietly,
　　　　　　in stillness...

　　　　　　"The sole cause for man's unhappiness
　　　　　　is that he does not know how to
　　　　　　sit quietly in his room."
　　　　　　　　　　　　Pascal

Be still,
　　　and listen to God

　　　　　Come Sunday...

Nineteen

Mystery of Life

Mystery on all sides!
    And faith
    the only star in this darkness and uncertainty."
                      Henri Amiel

    "So abandon yourself utterly to God
    and in this way,
    you will become truly happy."
                Henry Susa

We don't have the answers
    to all of life's questions,
    but victors of faith tell us
            it's OK...

    We sometimes don't even know
    the right questions to ask,
        but victors of faith tell us
            it's OK...

When your heart
    is filled to the brim
    with a love that is not of this world,
        there's a confidence,
    a peace,
        a sure faith
            that Someone knows the answers,
            and that we will know them one day,
        in faith,
        and in love...

there's no point to
agonizing and fretting,
or becoming obsessed about
what we don't understand...

Victors of faith
encourage us
to keep our eyes focused
on the true prize...
Sunday,
home,
and the
loving presence of God.

What *is* the purpose of life?
The lives of
victors of faith,
point to a common purpose:
knowing,
loving,
and serving the Lord...

each person's journey,
worthy of respect...
a divine mystery...

The best preacher is the heart;
the best teacher is time,
the best book is the world,
the best friend is God.

Hebrew proverb

Even in music
the mystery of life is echoed.

For example,

the searching jazz improvisational version
    of Duke Ellington's song, "Come Sunday,"
    played by Eric Dolphy on bass clarinet
    and Richard Davis on string bass,
          may at first
                present somewhat of a mystery
                to the novice listener...

    But this mystery is revealed in the beautiful words
                    of "Come Sunday,"
sung first by Mahalia Jackson and later by Esther Marrow,
    in recordings with the Duke Ellington Orchestra.

    Yet life's mysteries
        aren't always revealed in this life...

A wonderful friend to many,
    one surgical resident colleague
        was a very committed and loving person...

As he approached the end of
his many long years of arduous residency training,
    he expressed a longing for
        the purity of giving and service to others.
    He was not interested in the business
        or academic aspects of medicine...

    Yet this beloved young doctor
        suddenly and
        mysteriously
      jumped out of a top floor
          medical school building window
        to his death.

Why he did this,
   and why at a time
     when things seemed brightest for him,
          was—and still is—a surprise and a mystery
               to everyone…

     It was the kind of situation that wrings your heart.

     His family, friends and medical colleagues
felt confused,
        caught up emotionally by the total mystery
          of it all…
              no logical explanation,
              no scientific reason,
              no natural cause…

        clearly not understandable in human terms.

But many found great comfort
     in the words of a minister
     at a memorial service for
        the medical staff and friends
        of this young man.

     The minister began the service
with these simple words:

        "The mystery of life has been presented to us.
        We don't have all the answers,
        but we can take comfort that Someone does,
        and some day we will have them…"

Some things are just mysteries...
mysteries of life to which only God knows the answer,
indeed, the whole understanding of them is in His hands...
An ideology,
a code of ethics or philosophy alone,
is not enough—

we need a person to touch,
to communicate with,
someone who will understand...

we need a personal God,
and family,
and friends.

...always striving with human means
to reach spiritual ends—
through music,
friendships, words,
and holy reminders...

Building up strong defenses,
fortifying principles,
and character
are not the highest aspirations...
To be Christlike,
Christian and truly human,

*"And the longer you wait
to seek Him out,
the less you will know what life's about."*

"Prince of Peace"
Les McCann

To have needs,
          weakness,
     and suffering,
and to those in need,
       to be a friend…

          that is real.

"The Christian life is not a constant high.
    I have my moments of deep discouragement.
    I have to go to God with tears in my eyes,
    and say,
       'O God, forgive me'
       or 'Help me.'"

          Billy Graham

Sometimes
   victors of faith
       show their faith
       through contrast—
         standing steady and strong,
     when things seem to crumble
        and fall down
         around them…

      They are not mad at God
         for what they don't understand.

The Left Hand of God

Instead,
          their calm confidence points to a mystery,
                    a mystery of love...

Suffering is the most profound mystery of the universe,
and its mysterious purpose is found at the intersection of the
                    beams of the Cross—
          and every human pain
     has genuine value,
     united with Jesus' sacrifice of love...

                              in dying,
                    he destroyed death,
                         in rising,
                    he restored life.

     "Faith-illumined reason
          understands reality better than
                    naked reason...
          ...Lincoln saw the Civil War
          as a just chastisement
                    sent by God
                    for our sins."
                              Fulton Sheen

God often flies
          in the face of common sense
     in order to make sense—
               the mystery of the Lord...
Some say that
          he "writes straight
     with crooked lines"...

          "...Some people get burned out,
                    give up,
               accept defeat, and quit...

…Some get burned up,
            abandon faith,
                  and become cynical…

…Some just get brighter,
they glow with the golden light of inspiring faith—

            'Watch me world!
                  I may be tested, tried, and persecuted,
                  but I still trust God.'

They send out
            to the world
            an unspoken message
      that you can still believe in God
                  even when he is silent.

            The darker the suffering,
            the brighter the message that
                  this person shares with everyone."
                              adapted from Robert Schuller,
                              The Be (Happy) Attitudes

Mystery of beauty,
            of love,
of victory…

            "O ancient beauty,
                  ever new…"
                              St. Augustine

            Each of our spiritual journeys—
      a mystery of love,
                  of Sunday…

Twenty

Life is Short

A moment in time
might seem to last forever,

but the reality is,
life is short...

How short?

"We are on a very short journey.
Our human life is
a moment,
an astronomical time.

A mayfly lives two days.

You say,
'What a pitifully short life!'

Compared to the age of the
oldest living things,
which are the Sequoia trees in California,
the redwoods,

your life and mine
is much more like the life of a mayfly,
than it is like the life of a tree,
a Sequoia.

Compared to the age of the earth,
        your life and mine is almost indistinguishable
from that of the two-day mayfly.

                Life is terribly short.

                The world is 4 billion, 800 million years old—
                        What's your life and mine?

The older you are,
        the quicker you realize it is going by...

                        And the one thing that rescues us from all of
                                this is desire—

                                desire which can reach into eternity,
                                desire which can defy time,
                                desire which can reach up and
                                        grab the hem of God.

                                Human beings alone
                                have the capacity to
                                desire to live forever,

                        and that is what our desire must do.

If you don't,
        as you get older and you have desired
        only materialistic things,
                however beautiful,
                however elegant,
                perhaps however ennobling,
                        literature
                                or art
                        or what have you—
        as you get older,
                those things will get hollow.

A man who had
>much of the history of the world
>at his fingertips,
>>Winston Churchill,
>>>who did many things
>>>>of great power
>>>—he was a great man
>>>>of the world—
>>his last words were:
>>>'I'm so tired of it all'
>>>>'I'm so tired
>>>>>of it all.'

You see,
>desire does not go away—
>>desire gets buried alive
>>by all kinds of passing things—
>our whims, and vanities, and baubles..."
>>>>>>*Fr. Benedict Groeschel, C.F.R.*

How long do you expect to live on earth?
It could be longer or shorter than you expect.

>Consider that
>>during the time of Christ,
>>the median lifespan for a man was 30 years old...

>>but in 1903, it was 43 years old...

>>in 2003, in the United States, it was 78 years old...

>Yet even with a median lifespan of 78 years,
>that means that 50% of men died *younger* than age 78...

Imagine…
        If all the souls of the faithful departed
                and all the living, earthly souls
                were gathered together…
        We, the living, would be not only comparatively
                few in number.
                                We'd be lost in the crowd.

"We are tenants of time…"
                                Bishop Henry Mansell

Will you live to be 35,
                or 55,
                        or 90?

        Travel light on life's journey,
        life is too short
                to worry about possessions…

        Enjoy your job.
                Enjoy your life.
        Minimize stress.

                Enjoy each day the Lord has given you.

Does this mean
        "experience everything?"
        or mindlessly
                do whatever "feels good" at the moment?

                        What satisfaction is in that?
                        What legacy of value?

...loneliness,
      emptiness,
a lack of meaning
    and direction...

    Find the meaning
        of life,
    and discover
    true happiness...

            Life is short for all of us...

A star pitcher
    for the St. Louis Cardinals
    died suddenly in his sleep at age 33...
        on the day he was supposed to pitch
            against the Chicago Cubs.

    a 40-year-old
        devoted husband and father,
        a pillar of his community,
        and avid Washington Redskins fan
        died mid-speech
            on a podium...

    a 49-year-old man,
        concerned
        about his 80-year-old parents,
    just lay down on his couch one evening
        and
        passed away suddenly ...

"Live for today...
    You may not be around tomorrow."

            Ozzie Smith
            Hall of Fame baseball player
            St. Louis Cardinals

Some worry about
a diagnosis of
cancer,
yet they may not
die for 20 years from cancer,
if at all,
but they could
die tomorrow,
or in five years,
during a
heart attack...

and
if none of us
knows for sure
how long we have to live,
then what makes
us so different
from a patient with cancer?

Cancer victors
show us that
you have to
live life
like you don't know
if you'll be here tomorrow...

Life is short,
and you'll be together again
with those you love,
before you know it.

The length or shortness of your life
isn't what's important...

"To gain a new perspective
our questions must be simple
and profound.

What is important?
Who is important?
What are we going to do about it?"

Don Osgood

Life is short for all of us,
Sunday comes so soon...

Twenty-One

Follow Your Heart

Follow your heart
    and seek your greatest happiness.

        because
            if you follow your heart,

                you'll make the most of your talents.

                you'll aspire to greater levels
                    in whatever you choose to do,

                you'll be a happier person,

        and have faith,
                dear reader,
            that eventually it will lead you
            to the greatest happiness
                and wisdom
                        and sense of purpose
                        about why we are all here.

You may not be called
        to a long-term career
    as an athlete,
            or a musician...

But experiencing
        music and
        athletics are
                great first steps,

    because they teach you *how*
            to follow your heart.

                        Once you've gotten a taste

        of the exhilaration,

                of the hard work
                that went into it—
                        which never seemed like
                        hard work because you
                        loved it—

        of the satisfaction of achievement,
        and the joy of doing it with your friends,

                you won't want to
                settle for second-best...

    "Wheresoever you go,
    go with all your heart."
                            Confucius

So many colleagues
        tell similar stories of inspiration in their youth...

        ...some accompanied a mother, father,
                or grandparent to a cancer institute...

and it left a lasting positive impression on them.

Some people think
        that a cancer institute
        is a sad and depressing place,

    but nothing could be
    farther from the truth...

        Some colleagues recall that,
            as children,
            they were awed by the
                    spirit and enthusiasm
            of the physicians and patients
        facing an ultimate challenge,
            in this case,
                curing cancer.

            For one young boy,
                it was like Yankee Stadium
                and the Newport Jazz
                        Festival
                    combined.

    He was impressed by the
            spirit and love shown
            by everyone who came in contact
                with patients with cancer,
                no matter what their role was...

        It is clear that
    the richness of our lives
        can be measured
    not only by the heights we attain
                    in athletics
                    and music
                    and science,

but also
     by the degree
     that we help others
         less fortunate than ourselves.

     Choosing to help
patients with cancer is
     one way to contribute to other people…

     and the thought of
         becoming a doctor,
         seemed so unlikely then.

Now,
     so many years later,
     I've been privileged to be
         an appreciator of the lives
         and goodness
     of so many victors of faith.

When tragedies happen,
when bad things
     happen in the world,
     or in your life,
imagine the exponential power
         of all the good things that happen as well—

     Good things caused by
         people of faith who inspire others.
         who are not afraid,
       who live life with faith and heart,
         who give and live to the end…

These good things
happen every day,
in little ways,
all around the world,
among all peoples—

Think of the power of good
when these little things
are magnified
exponentially...

You should not do
what anyone else has done...

You should follow *your* heart
and *your* dreams...

perhaps a few dreams,

but you'll choose
from this menu of life
only several times...

don't be among those
who look back on their careers
with regret...

don't fall for the age-old folly
and slick marketing
that tells you
if you had more money,
you'd be happier...

and don't be afraid
to start *Now*...

Cancer victors,
victors of faith
tell us it's never too late
to begin…

"Don't aim at success—
        the more you aim at it and
        make it a target,
                the more you are going to miss it.

        For success,
                like happiness,
cannot be pursued;
                it must ensue…
                the unintended side effect
                        of one's personal dedication
                        to a cause greater than oneself…
        you have to let it happen
                by not caring about it…

                        in the long run…
                                success will follow you
                                precisely because you had
                                forgotten to think about it."
                                        Viktor Frankl

'Success is peace of mind,
which is a direct result of
        self-satisfaction in knowing
        you did your best
                to become the best
                you are capable of becoming."
                        John Wooden
                        Hall of Fame College
                        Basketball Coach, UCLA

What *are* the attributes of success?

> Dr. Kenneth Pelletier at the Stanford Center for
> Research in Disease Prevention at
> the Stanford University School of Medicine
> interviewed prominent
> men and women,
> from CEOs to actors,
> who represented
> prototypes of success and well-being.

> The findings are interesting...

> Material wealth and power,
> or exercise, or diet regimens
> held no assurance of
> success and well-being
> among those interviewed.

> Rather,
> those interviewed cited
> as attributes of success:

> Spirituality,

> Altruism,

> "Living in the now,"

> Caring relationships,

> Stress management, and

> Overcoming adversity.

> *Dr. Kenneth Pelletier*
> *"Sound Mind, Sound Body"*

One rainy day
      in April,
            several young doctors
      hurriedly exited the front doors
              of the cancer institute where they worked.

They were on their way from patient clinics to
            adjacent laboratories to meet with scientists.

An immaculate,
        gold-painted,
               Rolls Royce was parked
               at the front of the entrance...

This unusual site caught their attention and

          one of the young doctors recounted
          that it belonged to a young European man,
                             their age,

            who had arranged for the car
                 to be flown across the Atlantic
                in his private plane
          so that he could have it with him
                    during his trip to America.

     Some of the doctors
            wondered if they should be
            envious of this
               wealthy young man...

After all,
         they were only at the beginning of their
             long and demanding careers
                 they were often struggling financially,
                       and often fatigued.

But another doctor in the group spoke up...

"Don't be envious
of this man,"
the doctor said.
"This morning
he was diagnosed
with advanced cancer
that has spread throughout his body."

Each of these doctors silently paused
on this cold and rainy day,
and asked themselves:
"Am I where I want to be right now?"

Each of these young cancer doctors could say "yes,"
without hesitation.

They each knew
that they were pursuing
one of their dreams...
that they were following their hearts.

Do what you love
Love what you do,
or change your feelings about what you do...

"When I practiced medicine,"
observed a 90-year-old retired doctor,
"It was a calling."

"In the next generation,
it became a business...

and now, for some,
it's a hustle."

Some older musicians,
        some retired coaches
                and athletes,
and so many others
        may make the same observation about
                their professions...

In your pursuits,
        where do you find yourself?

Are you following your heart?

                One great actor,
                        who starred in thousands
                        of performances,
                                never failed to
                        exude childlike passion
                                for his work...

During a routine
        CT scan,
                to make sure that his aggressive form of cancer
                remained in remission,

        this actor told
                his physician that several other doctors
                recommended that he
                        discontinue his
                        busy performance schedule,

                They recommended that, instead,
                        he relax around his home
                        and do other things he
                                always wanted to do.

It sounded like reasonable advice,
but this actor
   was passionate in his response:

"Can you imagine that?
 What would you
  rather be doing
  than getting a standing ovation
    in front of 3,000 people every night?!"

It was very moving…

Despite thousands of performances,
   his passion never let up.

He was truly following his heart.

"If you are not happy,
 you have no one to blame
 but yourself."

a cancer victor and musician

"My Birdcage Needs a New Paper {Because My Parakeet's Already Read the One That's in There}"

Tony Trischka banjo
John Lanford lead guitar
Danny Weiss rhythm guitar
Paul Stomper bass clarinet
John Dancks bass
Mark Beebe drums
Bluegrass Light, Tony Trishka, Rounder Records, 1973

It's not always easy
>to follow your heart…

>The pearls of encouragement that follow
>>have been collected
>from cancer victors—

Don't be too discouraged
>>if changing trends or job market cycles
>>don't always go your way.

>>No one who has followed his or her heart had
>a timetable identical to the trends of the daily news…
>>that's why so many great athletes,
>>artists, and mothers waited on tables…
>>>but they did it with a sense of
>>>>meaning and direction.

Good things take time.
>>Don't be afraid to take the
>>slow road in this fast-paced world
>>and follow
>>>the beat of your own drummer.

>>When you need perspective,
>>>discover nature
>>>>and the great outdoors.

Don't be discouraged
>>by the changing winds of government.

>>>"Render unto Caesar
>>>>that which is Caesar's."

>>>Seek some of the riches which
>>>>no one can take away from you.

Don't be concerned
about the social status of
your life's work among your peers.

Social status is fickle
and changes all the time.

Let your happiness
and integrity
empower you
and give you status.

Don't be afraid of failure;
there are no perfect lives among us.

Victors of faith
show us that the
greatest fear in life is not death—
it's leading a life without heart.

"What will it profit when life is o'er,
Though great worldly wisdom I gain,
If seeking knowledge I utterly fail
The wisdom of God to obtain?"

Nelson

There are
       many special people
       who have followed their hearts.

       They have enjoyed many of the graces
           life has to offer—

           and their advice
       to their doctor,
           has always been poignant:

"I appreciate what you have
       done with your medicine and science,
but I hope that you too
    will take the time in your life
       to enjoy all the blessings
       I have had in mine."

       The greatest fear
    that people with cancer
    want to share with you,

           dear reader,

     is the fear
     that someday,
           when you look back at your life,
           you may realize that you
              didn't follow your heart,
           or at least try to follow it.

Will your life
      be another grain of sand
      in this hourglass of humanity,

          or will it be a pearl?

              ...follow your heart
                  to Sunday...

"*Come Sunday,
You'll come Sunday,
That's the day.*"
Come Sunday,
Duke Ellington

Twenty-Two

Come Sunday

God wants us to be happy,
        to enjoy the gift of Easter,
        to enjoy the gift of Sunday...

                to rejoice in
                      Spring after Winter...

            to faithfully accept
            the cross of Good Friday,

            so that we may
                anticipate
                the joy of the Resurrection,
                      the joy of eternal life...

Christ is risen,
        Indeed he is risen...

                Easter greeting and response
                among Eastern Rite Catholic
                and Orthodox faiths

        If you,
            dear reader,
        truly believe in Easter,
                and in the Resurrection,
    then it cannot help
        but change how you live,
            for it will spill over
                and transform
            every aspect of your life...

"All peoples should believe in eternal life—
Catholics, Eastern, Protestants, Jews,
Muslims, Hindus, Buddhists,
and seekers and searchers;
Jesus Christ is the gift of eternal life."

Fr. Benedict Groeschel, CFR

Sunday—
    a day of welcome rest,
    a time to nurture things that matter most
        a time to pray and worship,
        to spend with family and friends,
        to put away cares,
            relax,
               refresh,
           and re-energize,
        a time to nurture life-giving
              personal relationships…
        and at a deeper level,

Sunday—
   an assurance of faith,
     the resonance of
       the human heart for
    an eternal permanence
        to better things,
        for a life of endless peace,
           with no death,
      no tears,
      no sorrow,
      no suffering,
        no evil…
      but instead a boundless union
        of our life
          with pure life,
            profound love,
               unending joy
              and inner peace…

Sunday,
      the fulfillment
of a continuous journey,
      "on earth as it is in heaven…"

In the beautiful words of
Duke Ellington's song,
      "Come Sunday:"

"God, the Lord of Love,
  God almighty,
  God of power,

      Please look down
      and see my people through.

I believe that
      God put sun and moon up in the sky

      I don't mind the grey skies,
          'cuz they're just clouds passing by
The leaves of the valley—
      they neither toss nor spin,
          and flowers bloom
          and springtime birds sing.

Often we feel weary,
      but he knows our every pain…
Go to him in secret,
      He will hear your every prayer.

Oft from dawn to sunset,
      man works hard all day.
          Come Sunday,
          you'll come Sunday,
              that's the day."

The world needs more happy people—

    your smile is evidence of happiness...

"Do not make a home for yourself in the darkness,
    You have been created for the light of God's love."
Joseph Cardinal Bernadin

"In everyone's heart
    stirs a great homesickness."
Rabbi Seymour Siegel

"Home is the definition of God."
Emily Dickinson

"There are no limits
    to the truth you can know,
    to the life you can live,
    to the love you can enjoy,
        and to the beauty you can experience."
Fulton Sheen

But the words of this small book
convey merely
    one person's collage,
        one unique fusion of experiences,
      among the experiences of so many others...
    one person

who,
like so many others,
is an appreciator
of spirited musicians
and athletes,
and most especially
of cancer victors and
victors of faith—
patients with cancer and
those who serve in cancer centers,
who embrace the ordinariness of life
with faith,
who aspire and reach
beyond themselves,
and in doing so,
who inspire others.

"I have fought a good fight,
I have finished my course,
I have kept the faith."
II Timothy 4:7

"But there are also
so many other things...
which, if they were written every one,
the world itself,
I think,
would not be able to
contain the books
that should be written."
Ending of Gospel writings of St. John
John 21:25

When you multiply
                    this inspiration for living with heart
                    by all the victors of faith
                                    in the world today,
                    and then by all generations,
you will surely discover
                    evidence of love and hope
                    that is far, far greater
                    than any misfortune,
                                    pain,
                                    or evil
                    endured by any one person,
                    or by mankind...

For love is the greatest power in the world...
God's loving plan for
                    our universal and eternal happiness,
                                    for Sunday...

                    And why are we here?
                    What is the purpose of our life?

                                    ...to be one small
                                    part of that loving plan.

With Duke Ellington,
            with jazz musicians like
                            Eric Dolphy,
                    Richard Davis,
                            and John Coltrane,
            with many
                    great athletes and coaches,
                    and with all victors of faith,

may your heart and journey,
    your unique and endless song,
also resonate
    Come Sunday…

And during times of anxiety and uncertainty,
    may you also feel, deep within,
        the warm and triumphant glow of faith,
        that *in the very end, dear friend…*
            in the very end,
    you will be…

Victorious!

For eternity will be nothing like
    you have ever seen, heard or imagined—

    "Eye hath not seen,
        nor ear heard,
            neither hath it entered into the heart of man,
                what things God hath prepared
                    for them that love him."
                              I Corinthians 2:9

"From the beginning of the world
they have not heard,
     nor perceived with the ears:
the eye hath not seen, O God,
        besides thee,
what things thou hast prepared for them
          that wait for thee."
         Isaiah 64:4

"Let not your heart be troubled...
     I go to prepare a place for you.
And if I shall go,
    and prepare a place for you,
      I will come again,
        and will take you to myself;
        that where I am,
         you may also be."
        John 14:1-3

Suggested Listening
When words are not enough...

1. "Come Sunday"
Eric Dolphy {bass clarinet}
 with Richard Davis{b}
 "Iron Man", Metrotone, 1971
  -originally issued on Douglas International, SD 785, 1964

2. "Come Sunday"
Duke Ellington and his Orchestra
 Esther Marrow{voc},
 Duke Ellington{p}, Harry Carney{bs},
 Russell Procope{cl,as}, Johnny Hodges{as},
 Jimmy Hamilton{cl}, Paul Gonsalves{ts},
 Lawrence Brown{tr}, Buster Cooper{tr}, Quentin Jackson{tr},
 Charles Connors{tr}, Cootie Williams{t},
 William"Cat"Anderson{t}, Mercer Ellington{t},
 Herbie Jones{tr}, John Lamb{b}, and Louis Bellson{d}
 "Duke Ellington's Concert of Sacred Music" RCA, 1966;
 BMG France 1994

Duke Ellington and his Orchestra
 Mahalia Jackson{voc},
 Duke Ellington{p}, Cat Anderson{t},
 Harold Baker{t}, Clark Terry{t}, Ray Nance{t},
 Quentin Jackson{tr}, John Sanders{tr}, Britt Woodman{tr},
 Harry Carney{bs}, Paul Gonsalves{ts}, Bill Graham{as},
 Jimmy Hamilton{cl}, Russell Procope{cl,as},
 Jimmy Woods{b}, and Sam Woodyard{d}
 "Black, Brown, and Beige", Columbia Jazz, 1958

3. "Dear Lord"
John Coltrane{ts}
 with McCoy Tyner{p}, Jimmy Garrison{b}, and Roy Haynes{d}
 "A John Coltrane Retrospective: The Impulse Years"
 Impulse, MCA,GRP, 1992
  -originally issued on Impulse AS-9195, 1965

4. "WHAT WONDROUS LOVE IS THIS!"

Ramsey Lewis Trio
> Ramsey Lewis{p} with Larry Gray{b} and Ernie Adams{d}
> "Appassionata", Narada Jazz, 1999

5. "MERCY, MERCY, MERCY"

Cannonball Adderley Quintet
> Julian "Cannonball"Adderley{as}, Nat Adderley{c},
> Joe Zawinul{p}, Victor Gaskin{b},
> and Roy McCordy{d}
> "The Best of Cannonball Adderley: The Capitol Years"
> Capital Jazz, 1991
> -originally issued on Capitol ST 2663

6. "AMAZING GRACE"

Pete Fountain{cl}
> with Mike Genevay{tr}, Charles Lodice{d}, Oliver Felix{b},
> Tom Gekler{tr}, Bill Bachman{tr}, Ed Firth{tuba},
> Les Muscott{banjo}, Johnny Gimbel{fiddle},
> and Earl Vuiovich{p}
> "Swinging Blues", Ranwood Records, 1990

7. "SPIRITUALITY"

John Coltrane{ts}
> with Eric Dolphy{bcl}, McCoy Tyner{p},
> Reggie Workman{b}, and Elvin Jones{d}
> "A John Coltrane Retrospective: The Impulse Years"
> Impulse, MCA,GRP, 1992
> -originally issued on Impulse AS-10, 1961

8. "MY ONE AND ONLY LOVE"

Johnny Hartman{voc} and John Coltrane{ts}
> with McCoy Tyner{p}, Jimmy Garrison{b}, and Elvin Jones{d}
> "A John Coltrane Retrospective: The Impulse Years"
> Impulse, MCA, GRP, 1992
> -originally issued on Impulse AS-42, 1963

9. "OVER THE RAINBOW"

Stanley Jordan {g}
> with Kenwood Dennard{d} and Charles Moffet{b}
> "Stolen Moments", Blue Note, 1991

10. "THE LEFT HAND OF GOD"

Charlie Haden Quartet West
> Charlie Haden{b},Ernie Watts{ts}, Alan Broadbent{p},
> and Larance Marable{d}
> "Now is the Hour", Verve, Gitanes Jazz, 1996

11. "WADE IN THE WATER"

Ramsey Lewis Trio
> Ramsey Lewis{p} with Cleveland Eaton{b}, Maurice White{d},
> and Richard Evans{orchestra conducter}
> "Ramsey Lewis's Finest Hour", Verve, 2000
> -originally issued Cadet LP 776, 1966

12. "COUNTRY PREACHER"

Cannonball Adderley Quintet
> Julian "Cannonball" Adderley{ss} with Nat Adderley{c},
> Joe Zawinul{p}, Walter Booker{b},
> and Roy McCordy{d}
> "The Best of Cannonball Adderley: The Capitol Years"
> Capitol Jazz, 1991
> -originally issued on Capitol SKAO 404, 1969

13. "A LOVE SUPREME"

John Coltrane {ts}
> with McCoy Tyner{p}, Jimmy Garrison{b}, and Elvin Jones{d}
> "A John Coltrane Retrospective: The Impulse Years"
> Impulse, MCA,GRP, 1992
> -originally issued on Impulse AS-77,1964

14. "A LOTUS ON IRISH STREAMS"

The Mahavishnu Orchestra with John McLaughlin{g}
> with Jerry Goodman{v}, Jan Hammer{p}, Rick Laird{b},
> and Billy Cobham{d}
> "The Inner Mounting Flame", Sony/Columbia, 1971/1998

15. "WHAT A FRIEND WE HAVE IN JESUS"
Cyrus Chestnut {p}
> "Blessed Quietness: A Collection of Hymns, Spirituals,
> and Carols" Atlantic Jazz, 1996

16. "ON THE SUNNY SIDE OF THE STREET"
Dizzy Gillespie {t,voc}
> with Sonny Stitt{ts}, Sonny Rollins{ts}, Ray Bryant[{p],
> Tommy Bryant{b}, and Charli Persip{d}
> "Sonny Stitt: Verve Jazz Masters 50", Verve, Polgram, 1995
> -original issue on Verve MGV 826, 1957
> available on CD: 825 674-2

17. "THE CREATOR HAS A MASTER PLAN"
Pharoah Sanders {ts}
> with Leon Thomas {voc}, Lonnie Liston Smith {p},
> James Spaulding {flute}, Julius Watkins {French horn},
> Reggie Workman {b}, Richard Davis {b}, Billy Hart {d},
> Nathaniel Bettis {percussion}
> "Karma", Impulse! Records 1969/MCA 1995. AS-9181.

18. "PRINCE OF PEACE"
Les McCann{voc, p} and Joja Wendt{p}
> "Pacifique", MusicMasters, BMG, 1997

19. "LIFT EVERY VOICE AND SING"
Charles Lloyd {ts}
> with Geri Allen{p}, John Abercrombie{g}, Larry Grenadier{b},
> and Billy Hart{d}
> "Lift Every Voice", ECM, 2002

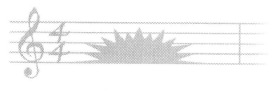

{as}alto saxophone, {ts}tenor saxophone, {ss}soprano saxophone,
{bs}baritone saxophone, {cl}clarinet, {t}trumpet, {c}cornet, {tr}trombone,
{g}guitar, {b}bass, {p}piano, {d}drums, {voc}vocal

Notes and Permissions

Scripture quotations are from the *American Standard Version.*

Coltrane and Dolphy:

John Maxwell. The Maxwell Leadership Bible, from the Introduction "God has already called you to lead", Nashville: Thomas Nelson Publishers, 1982.

Langston Hughes, as presented by J.C. Thomas, *Chasin' the Trane, The Music and Mystique of John Coltrane,* New York: Da Capo Press, Inc., a subsidiary of Plenum Publishing Corp., reprint of 1975 edition published by Double Day and Company, Inc., 228.

"Eric Dolphy grew up in…" and following paragraphs, including tax reference Cf. Alan Saul, Eric Dolphy Discography, http:/farcry.neurobio.pitt.edu/Discographies/ Ericdiscg.HTML and Vladimir Simosko and Barry Tepperman, *Eric Dolphy: A Musical Biography and Discography,* Washington: Smithsonian Institution Press, 1974, revised edition Da Capo Press, 1966. Permission granted.

"A friend from…practice his clarinet" Vladimir Simosko and Barry Tepperman, Ibid.

"At home [in California] I used to play …play with the birds." Eric Dolphy, "John Coltrane and Eric Dolphy Answer The Jazz Critics," *Down Beat,* April 12, 1962, an exclusive online extra, www.downbeat.com, 11/15/05. Down Beat is an internationally registered trademark of Maher Publications. Permission granted.

"Birds have notes in between our notes—…it's pretty." Ibid.

"…as I play more,…say they're wrong.", Transcription of Leonard Feather's interview with Eric Dolphy (no date, estimate 1964 according to Stephen Lasker), made available by Alan Saul, *Eric Dolphy Discography,* http://farcry.neurobio.pitt.edu/ Discographies/Ericdiscg.HTML, 11/15/05. Permission granted.

"Well, I can't say…running notes." Ibid.

"…while others socialized…Parker record." David Was, "Eric Dolphy: Saintly, Selfless and Underappreciated," http://www.addict.com/issues/1.12/Columns/ David Was Undrugged, 11/05/05. Permission granted.

"…perhaps the most important thing …give in return." George Avakian, a eulogy in the magazine *Jazz,* recounted by Vladimir Simosko and Barry Tepperman, in *Eric Dolphy, A Musical Biography and Discography,* Washington: Smithsonian Institution Press, 1974, revised edition Da Capo Press, 1996. Permission granted.

Story about Dolphy in lower Manhattan, David Was, "Eric Dolphy: Saintly, Selfless and Underappreciated," http://www.addict.com/issues/1.12/Columns/David Was Undrugged, 11/05/05. Permission granted.

"Eric Dolpy was a saint...in his playing." Charles Mingus, recounted in book by Vladimir Simosko and Barry Tepperman, *Eric Dolphy, A Musical Biography and Discography*, Washington: Smithsonian Institution Press, 1974, revised edition Da Capo Press, 1996. Permission granted.

"Once I saw Eric ...the night before." Richard Davis, Ibid.

"To me, jazz is ...in my music." Eric Dolphy, Ibid.

"This human thing in instrumental ...ordinary speech. " Eric Dolphy, Ibid.

"what had been an enthusiasm...spiritual lifeline." Ashley Kahn, *A Love Supreme, The Story of John Coltrane's Signature Album* , New York, Penguin Group, 2002, 8. Permission granted.

"[Coltrane's] real career spans...other musicians." David Wild, "A Brief Biography of John Coltrane," *David Wild's Wild Place*, http://www.wildmusic-jazz.com, 11/15/05, based on the biographical section of David Wild, *The Recordings of John Coltrane: A Discography*, 1979. Permission granted.

"During the year 1957...happy through music." John Coltrane, as presented by J.C. Thomas, *Chasin' the Trane, The Music and Mystique of John Coltrane*, New York: Da Capo Press, Inc., a subsidiary of Plenum Publishing Corp., reprint of 1975 edition published by Double Day and Company, Inc., 83.

"I will do all I can to ..." John Coltrane, beginning words from his poem *A Love Supreme*, Ashley Kahn, *A Love Supreme, The Story of John Coltrane's Signature Album*, New York: Penguin Group, 2002, 145. Permission granted.

"Coltrane is so different...Einstein of music." Willem de Kooning, as presented by J.C. Thomas, *Chasin' the Trane, The Music and Mystique of John Coltrane*, New York: Da Capo Press, Inc., a subsidiary of Plenum Publishing Corp., reprint of 1975 edition published by Double Day and Company, Inc., 89.

"For a long time Eric...to join us." John Coltrane, Ibid, 141.

"When you hear...capture it again." Eric Dolphy, Ibid, 171.

"The jazz band...them or not." Aaron Copland, Ibid, 194.

"Whenever I make a change...but go ahead." John Coltrane, Ibid, 194-195.

"John used to tell me how to listen...give it a critique." Cecilia Foster, cousin of

Elvin Jones' and wife of Frank Foster, as presented by Ashley Kahn, *A Love Supreme, The Story of John Coltrane's Signature Album*, New York, Penguin Group, 2002, 83. Permission granted.

"Sometimes I wish ...that's too bad." John Coltrane, as presented by J.C. Thomas, *Chasin' the Trane, The Music and Mystique of John Coltrane*, New York: Da Capo Press, Inc., a subsidiary of Plenum Publishing Corp., reprint of 1975 edition published by Double Day and Company, Inc., 205.

"Trane's musical approach ...fluidity and movement" Bradford Graves, Ibid, 224.

"Coltrane: They're [the performances] are long because...with the other band." John Coltrane, "John Coltrane and Eric Dolphy Answer The Jazz Critics," *Down Beat*, April 12, 1962. Permission granted.

"But when your set...long you play..." Ibid.

"If I feel like...quit, bow out." Ibid.

"What I'm trying to do...whole group." Eric Dolphy, Ibid.

"When John...for me" Ibid.

"...he came in, and...This helps me." John Coltrane, Ibid.

"Eric and I...years ago." Ibid.

"For all their theoretical...development..." John S. Wilson, Chuck Stewart. "Coltrane's 'Sheets of Sounds'" New York Times, August 13,1967, 107.

"In 1960 Coltrane...still to come" Ashley Kahn, *A Love Supreme, The Story of John Coltrane's Signature Album*, New York: Penguin Group, 2002, 6. Permission granted.

"Trane and Buddha...decent man." J.C. Thomas, *Chasin' the Trane, The Music and Mystique of John Coltrane* , New York: Da Capo Press, Inc., a subsidiary of Plenum Publishing Corp., reprint of 1975 edition published by Double Day and Company, Inc., 228-229.

"Coltrane's trademark...passionate and alive." Ibid., 224.

The following sources were also used for this chapter:

Alan Saul, Ph.D., *Eric Dolphy Discography*, http://adale.org/Discographies/ EDIntro.HTML, 11/15/05. Permission granted.

Milo Miles, "Eric Dolphy: Young Saint with a Horn," *SALON* www.Salon.com, January 13, 1996, a review of *Eric Dolphy: The Complete Prestige Recordings*. Permission granted.

Marshall Bowden. "John Coltrane; A Love Supreme". *Jazzitude, 2001,* http://www.jazzitude.com/Coltrane_supreme.htm, 11/15/05. Permission granted.

Editorial Reviews, *Publishers Weekly,* review on *A Love Supreme: The Story of John Coltrane's Signature Album,* by Ashley Kahn, August 26, 2002, Reed Business Information, a division of Reed Elsevier, Inc.: book: Viking Books, 2002. Permission granted.

"John Coltrane Biography," www.JohnColtrane.com, 11/05/05. The John Coltrane Foundation, Inc—Jowcol Music, California. Permission granted.

Emmett G. Price III, "The Development of John Coltrane's Concept of Spirituality and Its Expression in Music," The Berkeley McNair Journal, Vol. 3, Summer 1995. Permission granted.

The Endless Song:

"He [Coltrane] had experimented…humanistic values." Emmett G. Price III, "The Development of John Coltrane's Concept of Spirituality and Its Expression in Music," The Berkeley McNair Journal, Vol. 3, Summer 1995. Permission granted.

Fulton Sheen quotes. Permission granted by the National Office of The Society of the Propagation of Faith, New York.

Philip Toshio Sudo, *Zen Guitar,* New York: Simon and Schuster, 1999, p.169.

"I can only fly…Trust the catcher." Henri Nouwen, in a film documentary *Angels over the Net,* Spark Productions, 1995, courtesy of Gabrielle Earnshaw, The Henri J.M. Archives and Research Collection, Toronto, Ontario.

C.S. Lewis, *Voyage to Venus* by C.S. Lewis copyright C.S. Lewis Pte. Limited. Extract reprinted by permission.

C. S. Lewis, *Fernseed and Elephants* by C.S. Lewis copyright C.S.Lewis Pte. Limited. 1975. Extract reprinted by permission.

Be Not Afraid:

"God is at the heart…" Bishop Henry Mansell, diocese of Buffalo, author's notes.

Bearing the Cross of Uncertainty:

"On the Sunny Side of the Street," Dorothy Fields and Jimmy McHugh, ©1930 Shapiro, Bernstein, & Co. and Cotton Club Publishing for USA, control by EMI Music. International copyright secured. All rights reserved. Used by permission.

"When one of the [band]… I'll play at yours" Al Hirt, introduction to "Funeral March: Didn't He Ramble" on recording *Super Jazz I,* CBS Records, 1975.

"You have this idea…thing that happens." Eric Dolphy, ""John Coltrane and Eric Dolphy Answer The Jazz Critics," *Down Beat*, April 12, 1962, an exclusive online extra, www.downbeat.com, 11/15/05. Down Beat is an internationally registered trademark of Maher Publications. Permission granted.

"If I feel like…quit, bow out." John Coltrane, Ibid

Marv Levy, interview with author. Permission granted.

Coping with Tragedy:

"God whispers to …a deaf world." C.S. Lewis, *The Problem of Pain*. Permission granted.

Michael Flynn. Permission granted.

John Newton story, Cf. Al Rogers, "Amazing Grace: the Story of John Newton," http://members.ozemail.com.au/~grahampo/amazing_grace.html, http://www.flash.net/~gaylon/jnewton.htm, 11/15/05.

"Amazing Grace" by John Newton. 1779. Public domain.

Inspiration for a Lifetime:

Richard Parisi, interview with author. Permission granted.

"Jesus had to…each of us." Fr. Benedict Groeschel, C.F.R., "A Call to Conversion," *Seven Conferences on Cassette by Benedict J. Groeschel, CFR*, Boston: St. Paul Books and Media, 1989. Permission granted.

Thomas Moore, "Ballad Stanzas" in *Stagecoach Tours*, Arch Merrill, 1947, reprinted by Empire State Books, Interlaken, NY, 1991, 56.

Fulton Sheen quotes. Permission granted by the National Office of The Society of the Propagation of Faith, New York.

"Make heroic verse…" Josemaria Escriva, *Christ is Passing By*, Chicago, Illinois: Scepter Press, 1974, Foreword, 13. Permission granted by Studium Foundation, Madrid, Spain.

Live to the End, Give to the End:

"I can find God…" Josemaria Escriva, *Christ is Passing By*, Chicago, Illinois: Scepter Press, 1974, Foreword, 13. Permission granted by Studium Foundation, Madrid, Spain.

"All are called...transcendence of God..." Ibid.

"Which chapel...that one" Josemaria Escriva,as presented in *The Man of Villa Tevere – The Roman Years of Josemaria Escriva,* Nuevas Ediciones de Bolsillo, 2004, chapter 10.

Jack Stomper, interview with author. Permission granted.

Father Paul Keeling, Our Lady of Fatima Shrine, Lewiston, NY. Permission granted

Tara Parker-Pope and Kyle Pope, "In Death, an Appreciation of Work," *The Wall Street Journal,* Sunday edition, 9/02/01, p. B-10.

"...the church exists...other purpose." C.S. Lewis, *Mere Christianity.* by C.S. Lewis copyright C.S. Lewis Pte.Ltd. 1942, 1943,1944,1952. Extract reprinted by permission.

Fulton Sheen quotes. Permission granted by the National Office of The Society of the Propagation of Faith, New York.

Robert Schuller, *The Be (Happy) Attitudes.* Nashville: W Publishing Group, a division of Thomas Nelson, 1997. Permission granted.

The Spirit of an Athlete:

Fulton Sheen. Permission granted by the National Office of The Society of the Propagation of Faith, New York.

Theodore Roosevelt, "Citizen in a Republic" speech at the Sorbonne, Paris, April 23, 1910.

"Eating like a schoolboy...prefer his conversion" C.S. Lewis. *Fernseed and Elephants* by C.S. Lewis copyright C.S. Lewis Pte. Limited. 1975. Extract reprinted by permission.

"We know a case in which a violinist ...than his conscious" Viktor E. Frankl, *The Unconscious God: Psychotherapy and Theology.* (New York: Simon and Schuster, 1975), (Originally published in 1948 as *Der unbewusste Gott.* Republished in 1997 as *Man's Search for Ultimate Meaning*), cf. Dr. C. George Boeree, "Viktor Frankl," www.ship.edu/~cgboeree/frankl.html, 11/15/05.

Reggie Witherspoon, basketball coach, University at Buffalo, interview with author. Permission granted.

"Look around you...with your friends" Marty Glickman, opening ceremony speech at New York Empire State games, Syracuse N.Y., 1981, author's notes.

Marv Levy, *Where Else Would You Rather Be?* Champagne, Illinois: Sports Publishing L.L.C., 2004.

John Wooden, www.achievement.org/autodoc/page/woo0int-2, 9/25/05.

Life Beyond the Final Buzzer:

Dalai Lama, as presented by Richard Carlson, PhD, *Don't Sweat the Small Stuff...and It's All Small Stuff* New York: Hyperion, 1997, 230.

Yogi Berra, as presented in the NY Daily News, Sunday. 3/14/82.

"You know...with a win." Reggie Witherspoon, basketball coach, University at Buffalo, interview with author. Permission granted.

"Is this heaven? No, it's Iowa" Shoeless Joe Jackson to Ray Kinsella in movie *Field of Dreams,* book by W. P. Kinsella, screenplay by Phil Alden Robinson, Universal Pictures, 1989, www.imdb.com/title/tt0097351/quotes, 12/30/05.

Max Lucado, *When God Whispers Your Name,* Nashville: W Publishing Group, A Division of Thomas Nelson Publishers, 1994.

"My Uncle Alex Vonnegut..." Kurt Vonnegut, *Timequake,* New York: G.P. Putnam's Sons, 1997, 12. Permission granted.

"...'Our Town' by the late Thornton Wilder..." Kurt Vonnegut, *Timequake,* New York: G.P. Putnam's Sons, New York, 1997, 20-21. Permission granted.

Play Right Through It:

"Come Sunday" by Duke Ellington. Copyrighted 1946 {Renewed} by G. Schirmer. Inc. International copyright secured. All rights reserved. Reprinted by permission.

Padre Pio, *Quiet Moments with Padre Pio,* compiled by Patricia Treece, Michigan: Charis Books, Servant Publications, 1999, no. 86

Marv Levy, Hall of Fame and former Buffalo Bills coach, interview with author. Permission granted.

"If I feel like...quit, bow out." John Coltrane, "John Coltrane and Eric Dolphy Answer The Jazz Critics," *Down Beat,* April 12, 1962. Permission granted.

"Absolutely, I think...their burdens." Reggie Witherspoon, basketball coach, University at Buffalo, interview with author. Permission granted.

Losers in Disguise:

John Lennon, www.brainyquote.com/quotes/authors/j/john_lennon.html, 11/08/05.

Henry Kissinger on the virtues of being famous, as quoted in "Some Lively Thoughts About Boredom," a sidebar to an article by Roy Rivenburg, "A busy, noisy, stimulating world produces an ample supply of boredom," *Los Angeles Times,* February 22, 2003, p. E1

Ronald Dahl, as quoted in "Some Lively Thoughts About Boredom," a sidebar to an article by Roy Rivenburg, "A busy, noisy, stimulating world produces an ample supply of boredom," *Los Angeles Times,* February 22, 2003, p. E1

Roy Rivenburg, "A busy, noisy, stimulating world produces an ample supply of boredom," Los Angeles Times, February 22, 2003, p. E1

George Brett, Kansas City Royals, Baseball Hall of Fame induction, 7/25/99, www.baseballhalloffame.org/hof_weekend/1999/speeches/brett_george.htm. 11/12/05

"Sometimes I wish …heard it before…" John Coltrane, as presented by J.C. Thomas, *Chasin' the Trane, The Music and Mystique of John Coltrane,* New York: Da Capo Press, Inc., a subsidiary of Plenum Publishing Corp., reprint of 1975 edition published by Double Day and Company, Inc., 205.

"I have a captain…to the throne." Fulton Sheen. Permission granted by the National Office of The Society of the Propagation of Faith, New York. Permission granted.

Why Me?:

Introduction by Julian "Cannonball" Adderley to "Mercy Mercy Mercy" by Josef Zawinul, copyright 1966 by Zawinul Music, a division of Gopam Enterprises, Inc., Renewed, Used by permission. All rights reserved. See Suggested Listening.

Sermon. St. Mary's Church, Batavia, New York, Easter Sunday 1998.

I Am With You:

Fulton Sheen. Permission granted by the National Office of The Society of the Propagation of Faith, New York.

"Prince of Peace" by Les McCann, copyrighted 1983 by Jana Music. All rights administered by Irving Music, Inc. / BMI. Used by permission. All rights reserved

"...the church exists...for any other purpose." C.S. Lewis, *Mere Christianity* by C.S. Lewis copyright C.S. Lewis Pte.Ltd. 1942, 1943,1944,1952. Extract reprinted by permission.

"...In the end, every man... and how to give in return." George Avakian, a eulogy in the magazine *Jazz*, recounted by Vladimir Simosko and Barry Tepperman, in *Eric Dolphy, A Musical Biography and Discography*, Washington: Smithsonian Institution Press, 1974, revised edition Da Capo Press, 1996. Permission granted.

"If you go by feelings...it is a decision." Father John Corapi, author's notes, 5/12/02.

Realtime Spirituality:

"I said at the start of this year ..." Phil Jackson, basketball coach, Los Angeles Lakers as presented by Associated Press, Buffalo News, 6/14/02.

Dennis Prager. *Happiness is a Serious Problem*, New York: Reganbooks/ HarperCollins Publishers, 1996.

Max Lucado, *When God Whispers Your Name*, Nashville: W Publishing Group, A Division of Thomas Nelson Publishers, 1994.

Mahatma Gandhi, www.quotedb.com/authors/mahatma_gandhi/1, 10/25/05.

Chief Redjacket, Seneca Indian Chief in Western New York State, from an 1805 speech in reply to a speech delivered by the Rev. W Cram who told the Indians that he {Rev. Cram} was sent by their ancient friends to preach the Gospel among them. Chief Redjacket prefaced these remarks with "Go then and teach the whites. Select, for example, the people of Buffalo...Improve their morals and refine their habits. Make them less disposed to cheat Indians. Make the whites generally less inclined to make Indians drunk and to take from them their land." Copy of original transcription reviewed by author. Buffalo and Erie County Historical Society Archives, Mss.B00-2, Indian Collection, as transcribed by Dr. Cyrenius Chapin in 1805.

"There are no dogmas...one's neighborhood..." Josemaria Escriva, *Christ is Passing By*, Chicago, Illinois: Scepter Press, 1974, Foreword, 15. Permission granted by Studium Foundation, Madrid, Spain.

"I assure you...your everyday lives." Josemaria Escriva, *Christ is Passing By*, Chicago, Illinois: Scepter Press, 1974, Foreword, 13. Permission granted by Studium Foundation, Madrid, Spain.

Jimmy Carter, *Living in Faith*, Introduction, New York: Three Rivers Press of Crown Publishing Group, 2001. Previously published by Random House, 1997, 13.

"Patience...which we stand." Henri Nouwen, *Bread for the Journey,* January 5th entry, HarperCollins, 1997, www.thesunmagazine.org/Beams312.pdf , 11/12/05.

Simplicity:

John Ortberg, pastor, Willow Creek Community Church, South Barrington, Illinois. *The Life You Always Wanted,* Grand Rapids: Zondervan, 1997, 2002, 32.

"Live in...and depression." Fr. John Corapi, author's notes.

No Greater Love:

Fulton Sheen quotes. Permission granted by the National Office of The Society of the Propagation of Faith, New York.

Viktor Frankl story. Viktor E. Frankl, *The Unconscious God: Psychotherapy and Theology.* (New York: Simon and Schuster, 1975), (Originally published in 1948 as *Der unbewusste Gott.* Republished in 1997 as *Man's Search for Ultimate Meaning*), cf. Dr. C. George Boeree, "Viktor Frankl," www.ship.edu/~cgboeree/frankl.html, 11/15/05

Be Still:

Jimi Hendrix, as presented in *The Search for Peace: Release from the Torments of Toxic Forgiveness*, Robert S. McGee and Donald W. Sapaugh, Ann Arbor: Servant Publishers, 1996.

"The first job comes the very moment...out of the wind" C. S. Lewis, *Mere Christianity* by C.S. Lewis copyright C.S. Lewis Pte.Ltd. 1942,1943,1944,1952. Extract reprinted by permission.

Father Paul Keeling, Our Lady of Fatima Shrine, Lewiston, NY. Permission granted..

"In front of Rockefeller Center...and loving him" Cardinal Edward Egan, 2000, author's notes.

Mystery of Life:

"Prince of Peace" by Les McCann, copyrighted 1983 by Jana Music. All rights administered by Irving Music, Inc. / BMI. Used by permission. All rights reserved.

Fulton Sheen. Permission granted by the National Office of The Society of the Propagation of Faith, New York.

"...Some people get burned out, give up, ...shares with everyone" adapted from Robert Schuller, *The Be (Happy) Attitudes.* Nashville: W Publishing Group, a division of Thomas Nelson, 1997. Permission granted.

Life is Short:

""We are on a very short journey...and baubles..." Fr. Benedict Groeschel, C.F.R., "A Call to Conversion," *Seven Conferences on Cassette by Benedict J. Groeschel, CFR,* Boston: St. Paul Books and Media, 1989. Permission granted.

"We are tenants of time..." spoken by Bishop Henry Mansell, diocese of Buffalo, 2002, author's notes.

Ozzie Smith, baseball analyst's reaction to the sudden death of St. Louis pitcher Daryl Kile due to coronary artery disease on 6/23/02, CNN Sunday Morning, 6/24/02.

Follow Your Heart:

"Don't aim at success...think about it." Viktor E. Frankl, *The Unconscious God: Psychotherapy and Theology.* (New York: Simon and Schuster, 1975), (Originally published in 1948 as *Der unbewusste Gott.* Republished in 1997 as *Man's Search for Ultimate Meaning*), cf. Dr. C. George Boeree, "Viktor Frankl," www.ship.edu/~cgboeree/frankl.html, 11/15/05.

Dr. Kenneth Pelletier, *Sound Mind, Sound Body,* New York: Fireside book published by Simon and Schuster, 1994.

Come Sunday:

"All peoples should believe in eternal life..." Fr. Benedict Groeschel, C.F.R., "A Call to Conversion," *Seven Conferences on Cassette by Benedict J. Groeschel, CFR,* Boston: St. Paul Books and Media, 1989. Permission granted.

"Come Sunday" by Duke Ellington. Copyrighted 1946 {Renewed} by G. Schirmer. Inc., international copyright secured. All rights reserved. Reprinted by permission.

Fulton Sheen. Permission granted by the National Office of The Society of the Propagation of Faith, New York.

Photography Credits:

Cover. Beaver Meadows. Java, New York. Author.

Eric Dolphy in 1961. Permission granted by photographer Val Wilmer, London, England.

Stuart. Stuart Wheeler, Syracuse New York, circa 1950. Author collection.

Sun And Dark Clouds. Author.

Man and Woman Basketball Players. Paul Hokanson, photographer, University at Buffalo Athletics. Permission granted.

Little Girl. Virginia Clark {Stomper}, Barre Center, New York, circa 1930. Author collection.

Raymond. Permission granted by daughter Lorraine Maney.

Country Road. Beaver Meadows. Java, New York. Author.

Waterfalls. Akron Falls Park, Akron, New York. Author.

Grandfather Hobie, Leroy, New York, 1974. Permission granted by grandson and photographer Richard Greenaker, New Mexico.

Cover Design and Page Layout:

Cathy Hofher

Notes

Notes

Notes

Notes

PAUL C. STOMPER, M.D. grew up in Batavia, NY. Dr. Stomper, a musician and sports enthusiast, studied at the Berklee College of Music and graduated from Syracuse University and Upstate Medical College. He has served full-time on the faculties of Harvard Medical School at the Dana-Farber Cancer Institute and Massachusetts General Hospital Cancer Center (1982-1989) and Roswell Park Cancer Institute (1989-2004). Dr. Stomper has authored over one hundred papers in peer-reviewed medical journals and authored the book, Cancer Imaging Manual.

KAREN A. WALKER is a journalist and editor based in San Juan Capistrano, California.

It is hoped that this book may inspire performance and arrangement by musicians and composers.

To order online:
www.buybooksontheweb.com
Call toll-free (877)buy-book